WHEN THE BOSS IS WRONG

A senior civil servant, **Dr Sibichen K. Mathew**, is also a leadership trainer, blogger, sociologist, and policy researcher. He is a post graduate in Public Policy and Management from Indian Institute of Management, Bangalore. He secured first rank from the University of Kerala in MA(Sociology), A Grade for MPhil from the Jawaharlal Nehru University, New Delhi, and PhD from the Bharathiar University, Coimbatore. He received LLB Degree from the Karnataka State Law University where he was a college topper and a rank holder. He is a recipient of the UGC Research fellowship, and has been awarded gold medals from the University of Kerala, National Police Academy and National Academy of Direct Taxes. Dr Mathew belongs to the 1992 batch of the Indian Revenue Service (IRS) and is currently Advisor, Telecom Regulatory Authority of India. His website is www.sibichen.in and he can be reached at sibi5555@gmail.com.

WHEN THE BOSS IS WRONG

Making and Unmaking of the Leader within You

Sibichen K. Mathew

RUPA

Exclusive interviews with:
Kiran Mazumdar-Shaw, Chairperson, Biocon
S.D. Shibulal, Co-Founder, Infosys Ltd
Marten Pieters, MD and CEO, Vodafone India
Wayne F. Cascio, Professor, The Business School, University of Colorado

Illustrations by:
Sajjive Balakrishnan, Manjul
and
Cartoons & Comics Syndicate

*Dedicated to all bosses:
yours and mine,
past, present and future*

Published by
Rupa Publications India Pvt. Ltd 2015
7/16, Ansari Road, Daryaganj
New Delhi 110002

Sales centres:
Bengaluru Chennai
Hyderabad Jaipur Kathmandu
Kolkata Mumbai Prayagraj

Copyright © Sibichen K. Mathew 2015

All rights reserved.
No part of this publication may be reproduced, transmitted, or stored in a retrieval system, in any form or by any means, electronic, mechanical, photocopying, recording or otherwise, without the prior permission of the publisher.

The author's views are personal and the opinions expressed in this book are the author's own and the facts are as reported by him which have been verified to the extent possible, and the publishers are not in any way liable for the same.

P-ISBN: 978-81-291-3682-4
E-ISBN: 978-81-291-3638-1

Eleventh impression 2024

15 14 13 12 11

The moral right of the author has been asserted.

Printed in India

This book is sold subject to the condition that it shall not, by way of trade or otherwise, be lent, resold, hired out, or otherwise circulated, without the publisher's prior consent, in any form of binding or cover other than that in which it is published.

CONTENTS

Preface	ix
Acknowledgements	xi
Introduction	xiii
Prologue: Before you begin	xvii

1. You are what your boss is — 1
2. The nasty bosses — 5
3. The 'runaway' boss — 11
4. Mr Boss, you are petty! — 15
5. When the boss is a 'snooperviser' — 19
6. The time bandits — 26
7. The towering bosses — 30
8. Working with 'hyper-intelligent' bosses — 35
9. The fault-finders — 39
10. Mr Boss, are you out of your mind?! — 43
11. Who will bell the boss? — 49
12. You do the work; boss takes the credit — 53
13. Unethical bosses — 58
14. The coterie rules; not the boss — 65
15. The chatterbox — 68
16. The please-all boss — 73
17. Where there is a will, there is a load! — 77
18. Why doesn't the boss smile? — 82
19. Predecessor bashing: What foolish bosses do! — 86
20. Coping with a young boss — 90
21. Coping with an old boss — 94
22. The braggarts — 100
23. Mr Boss! Don't always look up. Look down too! — 105

24. The archetypical bosses	110
25. The jealous boss	115
26. When bosses are good slaughterers	119
27. The boss: The profane self and the sacred self	124
28. The boss by default	128
29. The pathetic apathetic boss!	132
30. When the boss becomes a CEO: The Chief Ego Officer	138
31. The boss and your health	146
32. Bossing after bossing hours	150
33. Appraisal: The boss's ammunition and the subordinate's nightmare	154
34. Bosses and the Bathsheba syndrome	162
35. Boss speaks in Latin; we hear Greek	168
36. The puppet has a long tenure	176
37. Bosses and the image-makers	180
38. Which animal are you and your boss?	184
39. The inscrutable boss! You are being watched	189
40. How creative are you and your boss?	194
41. Boss leaves; bomb explodes	199
42. The Messiah returns	204
43. The bosses and the expats	209
44. The best leave; the worst stay	217
45. Boss is from Mars; you are from Venus	221
46. Is the family the shock absorber or the shock trigger?	227
47. Don't count just the successes; count the tears too	231
48. The corporate bureaucratic bosses and emotional intelligence	235
49. Static rules and rocky bosses	243
50. Ineffective bosses create ineffective organizations	247
Epilogue: Thank your boss for making you a good leader	254
Score Analysis	255
Notes	260

PREFACE

The primary stimulus for writing on the theme of this book was the experiences shared by people who had interacted with me and my own personal observations. The focus of this book is bosses at workplaces, though one could have bosses in other domains as well, including in one's own family! However, one can't base the book on information shared or observed privately. So I undertook what I proudly prefer to call 'systematic inquiry'.

My review of writings on leaders in organizations across the world indicated the general tendency of searching and projecting 'ideal types'. The pilot study undertaken by me substantiated my assumption that true learning can take place not by looking at the right traits, but by analysing the wrong ones. Looking at the wrong and its negative consequences is more meaningful and convincing than going after the right and searching for its positive results.

More often than not, it is neither a pleasant nor a welcome experience to tell a colleague that he is wrong. Although he might be more receptive if the consequences similar wrongs had for him or other colleagues or the organization were to be pointed out. One could learn lessons from such examples. Thus the focus in the book is on instances where the boss was wrong. I have presented in this book 50 different dimensions of bad leadership and their ramifications for people and organizations. There is also an attempt to suggest certain precautions and prescriptions for individuals (in their roles both as team members and as bosses) and some precepts for the organizations concerned. These can be applied to entities of any type, size, or genre: including companies, government organizations, educational, charitable and religious institutions, family businesses, voluntary associations, and clubs.

The bosses you come across in this book might remind you of your own bosses, or even yourself. This book will put you on your way to becoming a successful leader. Happy reading!

ACKNOWLEDGEMENTS

What do I have that I did not receive?

I am indebted to the hundreds of unnamed people who shared their experiences with me and provided invaluable inputs for this book.

I am grateful to Wayne F. Cascio, Kiran Mazumdar-Shaw, S.D. Shibulal, and Marten Pieters for their interviews and valuable inputs.

There are many individuals who held my hands during this journey. K.P. Karunakaran, my first boss, took pains to sift through book—separating the sense from the nonsense—and prevented me from sounding like an uncharitable boss-baiter. Sajjive Balakrishnan, my friend and a gifted cartoonist, who worked on my earlier books as well, along with renowned cartoonist Manjul and his team gave creative and humorous expression to my ideas. I fondly acknowledge the valuable suggestions from Sebastian Joseph and Sindhu John after reading the drafts. My sincere thanks to my teacher, Professor L. Prasad (IIM Bangalore) and my dear friends Ajai Pratap, Gangadharan, Hari Krishnan, Murali M., Muralidhar Krishnamurthy, Narendra Naik, Srinivasa Rao and the readers and subscribers of my blog 'Cyber Diary' for their valuable inputs.

I am grateful to Dibakar Ghosh and the team at Rupa Publications India for bringing this book to you.

Above all, I thank Rani, for being my inspiration, always.

INTRODUCTION

Everyone in this world is accountable to someone else in some way. Both leaders and leadership have existed from the beginning of human existence, and have provided direction and progress to society. Though the earliest theocratic societies thought leaders to be of divine origin, later it was found that leadership is a product of social experience[1] and is a universally developed attribute. Understandably, leadership became one of the most researched areas in social sciences initially and later became the key subject matter in the newly evolved discipline of management science. As Ralph M. Stogdill[2] has put it, there are almost as many different definitions of leadership as there are people who have tried to define it.

Across the world, there are thousands of institutes and tens of thousands of trainers in the thriving leadership development industry. There is also a plethora of theoretical and empirical studies and books on leadership, though all of them talk of the same thing in different ways. The main reason for this is the homogeneous approach to studying leadership. Barbara Kellerman rightly observed that the 'contemporary leadership field is an American product—an American seed planted in American soil and harvested by American scholars, educators and consultants'.[3] Thus, most of the leadership theories have been based upon the concept of there being one 'best' leadership model, or as I call it, one 'west' leadership model. Such a model, if applied without considering the time, space and organizational type, could become the 'worst' leadership model! Even today, scholars and management experts tend to demonstrate a large number of cases and illustrations of ideal leadership.[4] But the fact remains that there is no permanently ideal model of leadership. Further, management theories on this subject are often built on the premise that all individuals are rational beings who take decisions based on a cost-benefit analysis.[5] However, the assumption that ideal leaders are always logical, rational, scientific and coherent is incorrect. This misconception has emerged due to non-recognition of leaders' 'basic emotional traits' or the social context in which they grew up and operate.

The psychodynamic perspectives of leadership that had roots in the approaches of Freud, Jung and their theories of psychology[6] primarily originated with an analysis of ego states. Allport's trait theory of leadership could explain the influence of cardinal traits, central traits and secondary traits that affect leadership behaviour in different situations.[7] Later, Eric Berne propounded three ego states that are observable: Parent, Adult, and Child. Many scholars[8] of leadership have liberally drawn from these perspectives. One of the key assumptions in this approach is that the response of the leader is based on his own emotional status built on past experiences. There are many criticisms on the leading approaches to the study of leadership.[9] Undoubtedly, we need a synthesis of various theoretical perspectives to analyse the concept of leadership. An attempt in this direction was made by Bruce Avolio.[10] In integrated perspectives, even when the focus is on personality traits or behavioural patterns, barring a few exceptions, almost the entire literature in the area of leadership ultimately focused on 'efficiency' and 'performance' of the managers. Adequate attention is rarely given 'goodness' or to 'nastiness' as the crucial attributes for acceptability or disapproval of a leader by the people functionally or structurally under them.

Unlike focusing on one aspect of leadership: leader, follower, or organizational context, the attempt here is to analyse leadership by focusing on the 'boss–team member relations'. Such a relational approach can provide very valuable insights into various leadership styles and their acceptability in varied organizational settings. It is said that leadership is very much in the eyes of the followers. Yet, very few books have focused on the views and perceptions of followers to analyse patterns of leadership.[11] My attempt here is to identify the mistakes and failures of bosses as perceived by followers through direct observance of their approaches and behavioural patterns within the organizations. To succeed as an executive, manager, or leader, one should not only know how to manage a team, colleagues, and external stakeholders, but also their relationships with the bosses. Therefore, the nature of perception of the bosses and the determining factors in others' attitude and behaviour towards them are important areas in the understanding of leadership dynamics within an organization.

Bitter experiences can have a profound impact on one's understanding of a situation, of the people involved and also of oneself. They can also teach one lessons for the future much more forcefully and convincingly than any training programmes, advice or personal exposure to best practices and exemplary behaviour. This book focuses on how bosses could be bad role models and how the mistakes, failures, and negative traits perceived in them can become lessons in leadership for the teams around and under them.

The data for this book was collected in three phases: first, through a comprehensive questionnaire filled in by 1000+ employees and containing both closed and open-ended questions; second, through detailed conversational interviews with more than 100 individuals who shared their personal experiences; and third, based on the data collected in the first two phases, interviews were conducted with 10 leaders of large organizations who have been in those positions for a considerable period of time.

Thus the primary data has been gathered through my personal interactions and interviews with various executives, managers and CEOs from a range of sectors and industries. While some CEOs chose anonymity, others allowed me to use their names, some of them being: S.D. Shibulal, co-Founder, Infosys; Wayne F. Cascio, professor at the Business School, University of Colorado; Kiran Mazumdar-Shaw, chairperson, Biocon; and Marten Pieters, head, Vodafone-India.

Prologue

BEFORE YOU BEGIN

The word 'Organization' is used in this book as an inclusive label to refer to all types of entities, namely, companies, firms, charitable institutions, associations, government and public sector enterprises, family businesses and any other similar entities.

The word 'Boss' is used in this book as a generic label to refer to any person superior in position or role in relation to your profession or position. No other term was found appropriate enough to clearly depict the diverse characteristic traits, attitudes, approaches and behavioural patterns of those who are at the helm. Further, the nomenclature 'boss' is distinct from 'leader' or 'manager'. All managers can be bosses but all bosses might not be managers. Similarly, all bosses or managers cannot be called leaders.

The term 'Team Member' refers to any person who works under a boss, directly or indirectly.

Pseudonyms have been used in place of real names of individuals and organizations in the anecdotes and narrations in order to prevent possible embarrassment and to maintain anonymity, except in the interviews reproduced in the book.

Only ubiquitous and frequently occurring illustrations, anecdotes and examples have been selected for explaining various dimensions. Exceptional and odd incidents or behavioural patterns are not narrated and analysed in the book since they are not purposive in drawing conclusions or suggesting prescriptions that are generally applicable.

The book is divided into 50 very short chapters; read each of them slowly. Each chapter has its own climax and focuses on a unique theme, and you may read them in the order given or at random. However, self-assessment tests, wherever given, are connected to the content dealt with in adjacent chapters.

There are many exercises inside the book. Have a pencil and a writing pad ready (if you do not wish to scribble on the book or want to share it with others) while reading each chapter. You can check and assess your responses by referring to the 'Score Analysis' given at the end of the book.

Theories and scholarly references are given only in unavoidable instances so as to maintain the flow of the thought process and self-assessment. However, you are encouraged to refer to the resources to get more clarity, if required, while reading.

Preferred neutral terms are used to avoid sexist terms as much as possible. However, in most places the pronoun 'he' and in some places the pronoun 'she' and their derivatives are used. They signify both genders and transgender.

1

YOU ARE WHAT YOUR BOSS IS

IN AN IDEAL world, bosses can't ever be wrong, though the reality is quite different. Further, if your boss is wrong, you are at risk of being so as well. This is because there is a distinct possibility that he has had an indelible influence on you and you might be emulating him. Therefore, before we begin dissecting the wrongs of bosses in the subsequent chapters, you should be aware of the need for introspection on who you are and how you behave with people within your organization.

Do you hate your boss?

Because he is unapproachable, cynical, pessimistic, suspicious, rude or impatient?
   For the way he behaves, speaks, responds and reprimands, and for his lifestyle?

Do you ignore your boss?

Because he is stoic, demotivating, indifferent or uninvolved?
   For being indecisive, irresponsive and impersonal?

Beware!

There is a risk that you have or could become just like your boss!
   Whether you love, hate or ignore them, one thing is certain. You could have consciously or unconsciously absorbed some of the personality traits of your boss. The more you work with him, the more your personality can get synchronized with his. This process would not necessarily happen contemporaneously; it could continue

to show up even after you have left your boss or he has left you. Though you may have worked with many bosses, some of their traits could hang on to you for a long time!

This synchronization can take place not only in the spectrum of behavioural patterns, but also in attitude, vision, reasoning and emotional attributes. You might begin to copy the way your boss speaks, reprimands, praises, and advises and even the way he writes or walks.

His words and jargon, tones and accent can get ingrained in your own speeches and responses gradually. His favourite quotations, punch lines, illustrations and jokes often become your quotations, punch lines, illustrations and jokes.

You may even tend to imitate his sitting posture, and start responding to the telephone (including the way you say 'Hello'!) the way he does.

You might think that this observation is too farfetched, but it is a reality no one likes to admit.

Your lifestyle changes

You might pick up his interests and hobbies. You might try your hand at golf if he happens to be a 'golfaholic'.

Even your food habits might get influenced, though the extent of this influence would depend on how closely you have moved with your boss. There is a possibility of you switching to his brand of beverages, cigarettes or food products.

This influence can also be seen in the way a person dresses and grooms himself. Even when you hate that loose, untucked shirt of your boss, you might make occasional unconscious attempts to dress the same way.

Going further, I would say, there is a possibility of similarity in physical attributes as well. Therefore, one would not be surprised to see a subordinate transforming from a person with a concave stomach to one with a protruding belly under the influence of a paunchy boss. When emotions, behaviour and habits synchronize, there could be a proportionate impact in the physical and physiological realms.

Leo, a senior manager at an investment company, was very relaxed when he worked under a boss who was an easygoing kind of person. The latter was not bothered about meetings, reviews and deadlines. He was thought to be an 'ideal' person to work under. As time passed, Leo became very cool, relaxed and also slow in his work. Once he got elevated to the post of the boss, he continued to behave like his ex-boss. He could not motivate his team members, and his sluggishness had a debilitating effect on the entire team.

When aggressive norms are displayed, aggressive behaviour will also flow downward.[12] Aggressive bosses could pave the way for team members becoming aggressive, and as a result the organization can be perceived as an aggressive one.

How to take the best and reject the worst traits of your boss?

Is it impossible to insulate yourself totally from the influence of bosses? In a way, it is. But with strong willpower and discipline, you can train yourself to not be influenced unfavourably.

Your boss should be your role model, but only to a certain extent. You need to be wise enough to emulate only those elements of his personality that would make you more efficient, successful, happy, peaceful and creative. Alongside, there should be deliberate attempts to not follow or be influenced by his negative traits. How can this be done?

First and foremost, you need to observe your boss closely. You can evaluate what aspects of his personality are positive, vibrant, productive and exemplary. This can be gauged easily provided you get a chance to move closely with him.

Secondly, you must get feedback about your boss from those who have dealt with him at different levels and in varied situations. Their perceptions about him and a close examination of the influence he had on them would give an insight into his generally accepted traits. You can also collect a feedback from his previous team, which would give you a good enough idea for you not to be mesmerized by certain attitudinal and behavioural patterns.

Thirdly, you need to draw a line somewhere in the interactions. By all means, cultivate or nurture a relationship with your boss, but don't go beyond a limit to develop a very personal relationship. Bosses, by and large, are not comfortable with such intrusions.

Fourthly, don't ever think that your boss is a 'perfect' role model, even if you have become an ardent fan. You need to understand that apparent perfections can become clear imperfections in different situations and times.

Lastly, you are a real success when your boss picks up some of your virtues, traits or lifestyle changes and emulates the same. Thus, the 'moral of the story' is that there should be mutuality, reciprocity and exchange in a boss–subordinate relationship.

2

THE NASTY BOSSES

WHAT, ACCORDING TO you, is the crucial factor that brings happiness in one's job? Is it the pay, nature of work, work conditions, bosses, colleagues, subordinates or clients?

Sam is an exceptionally brilliant management professional. He was working in a multinational software company in a senior position; a cheerful and enthusiastic guy. The other day when he met me at a function, he said, 'I am thinking of leaving my job.'

I took him aside and asked, 'I'm sure you have got a hefty bank balance now because of your savings. But are you sure you don't want to work any more?' He said, 'It is not that I dislike my job. But for the last three years, I have been suffering because of a very nasty boss. I think he hates me as much as I hate him. He does not appreciate my achievements. He does not give me due recognition or respect; instead, he likes to snub me in meetings in the presence of my own team members.'

Sam is not alone. There are many who leave lucrative assignments to get away from nasty bosses. Jay Carter[13] wrote that nasty bosses can wreak havoc in one's life at work and at home, and therefore, one has to take concrete steps to stop getting hurt by them without stooping to their level.

Nastiness by bosses can be attributed to many factors. It is a unique personality trait where an individual behaves nastily with people he or she doesn't like. The most common reasons for this can be jealousy, mistrust, prejudice, their own bad experiences with their bosses or others, and so on.

The presence and perception of nastiness can result in conflicts and strains within an organization. In their paper, Tanya L. Chartrand, Amy N. Dalton and Fitzmons (2006)[14] elaborated the concept of reactance originally developed Thomas Hammock and Jack Brehm (1966),[15] and found that high-reactant individuals unconsciously and unintentionally reject the goals they associate with relationship partners and instead, pursue opposing goals. As such, they conclude that individuals behave in opposition to the goals of the significant others when they perceive the latter to be controlling.

Nasty bosses can thus make the workplace very difficult to be in, and cause excessive incivility in organizations. Employees are also not able to contribute their best under them. Christina Boedker conducted a study[16] on 5600 employees at more than 70 Australian companies and found that leadership has the greatest correlation with firm productivity and profitability. According to her research, a critical part of increasing workplace productivity is having a great boss.

I met Sen during a train journey. I had observed the middle-aged man reading *Great short stories of the world* for many hours while most of the other passengers were sleeping or working on their laptops. We chatted for a brief period before the train reached its destination. He told me he had been working as a wholesale dealer of electric goods for two years, after being the vice-president of a well-established company. When I asked him why he had quit his job and how he felt in his own business, he laughed. 'You must have seen how much I enjoyed this train journey, reading my favourite books? I think I lost 18 years of my precious life working for organizations that squeezed me. After my experience with the last boss I decided to quit. He used to ask me a lot of nagging questions, like "How many times do you go to the cafeteria to have coffee?", "Why do your wife and children call you while you are at work?", "How could you plan a holiday when the company is struggling to reach its target?" He wanted me to work as his bonded labourer.'

When an officer of a government department was asked why she felt her boss was nasty, she said, 'I was always a sincere officer. I used to contribute my best at work, giving excellent results. But on one occasion my boss insisted that I stay in office to prepare reports even though my son was seriously ill and was hospitalized. He didn't care that I was a single mother and there was no one else to take care of my child. From that day on, I started hating my boss.'

A senior programme designer with an IT firm said, 'My boss is a leech. He sucks till the last drop. After assigning any complex project, he chases me from the next day, saying, "At any cost, you need to complete this immediately." He won't let me go home till late at night. In my career of about 10 years with this organization, I have spent more time with my boss than with my family.'

Chess masters

Many executives complain that the strongest weapon bosses use against them is the threat of transfer. There are bosses who behave like chess masters by treating their juniors as nothing more than pawns on a chess board. Unfortunately you can't choose your bosses, so what is the remedy? Sincere attempts to understand the personality traits of your boss must be made in such cases, so as to try not to get hurt by his responses or temperament. You also need to be careful in responding to his uncharitable remarks and unpleasant responses.

Prescription for you, the boss

Do you want to be the Hitler of your organization? If not, respect those who report to you. They expect you to be a responsible, gentle, fair and empathetic leader rather than a rigid, inhuman, unjust or arrogant one. Why would you want to earn all those negative vibes from people around you?

Precaution for you

Often, we fail to appreciate and understand the situational constraints that the boss faces that push him to act in a particular way. It is imperative that you should try to understand these problems, pressures, targets and goals set for him by the organization. This will help reduce the intensity of your emotions in response to his callous attitude.

Further, try to maintain a cordial, frank and honest relationship with the boss, in spite of his nastiness. This will work wonders and you will probably find a change in his approach over time. Maintaining a distance or engaging in open rebellion is not at all a remedy here, as this will only worsen the situation.

In extreme and intolerable situations, you should not hesitate to report the behaviour of the boss to a level higher in the hierarchy, especially if your organization has a confidential feedback system in place.

Precept for the organization

The behaviour of bosses has a far-reaching impact on the organization and its team members. Before hiring someone, go beyond their CV or references from former employers. Instead, take pains to get data from former team members about their behaviour as a boss. This might be a bit difficult, but it is worth the effort.

In case there are already such bosses in your environment, protect your organization by establishing a 360-degree appraisal system that attaches significant weightage to feedback from subordinates.

The signs of recovery

Good leaders attract and retain the best talent. They also create a culture of mutual respect for each other within the organization.

Is your boss a bully?

The word 'bully' is chosen here though there are many other descriptions people use to refer to nasty bosses, such as creep, jerk, tyrant, Hitler or sadist. 'Bully' represents and connotes all the negative elements we see in such bosses. See some difficult bosses depicted in movies. They are real indeed!

Horrible Bosses
For many people, their bosses are simply 'horrible'! Incidentally, there is a famous comedy movie with the same title about three employees who have had enough of their bosses. Nick (Jason Baterman), Kurt (Jason Sudeikis) and Dale (Charlie Day) decided to kill their respective bosses in *Horrible Bosses,* directed by Seth Gordon and released in 2011. They consult a conman and also a professional killer to get rid of their abusive, controlling and manipulative bosses. Though the plot fails, the movie demonstrates how frustration, agony and anger grow uncontrollably in an unpleasant work environment.

9 to 5
If in *Horrible Bosses* we find the revenge of three men against their bosses, in the 1980 American film *9 to 5*, three women employees fight against their nasty, exploitative 'boss from hell' (Dabney Coleman). In the film, one can see how the three employees Judy (Jane Fonda), Violet (Lily Tomlin) and Doralee (Dolly Parton) overthrow their authoritarian, 'sexist, egotistical, lying, hypocritical bigot' boss.

The Devil Wears Prada

Based on the novel by Lauren Weisberger, the movie *The Devil Wears Prada* depicts a tyrannical boss. Miranda Priestley, a bullying magazine editor, has all the characteristic features of an intolerant boss. Some of the characteristics she displays are as follows:

- Treats employees as servants
- No reward for extra work
- Dictates work without explaining how to do it
- Verbal abuses and personal insults

Is your boss, too, a bully at the workplace?

Yes, if the boss is

- Very aggressive with employees
- Verbally abuses them
- Shouts very often
- Makes insulting remarks
- Humiliates members in front of others
- Oversupervises work
- Changes the work parameters very often
- Fixes unrealistic targets

…and other similar behaviour.

3

THE 'RUNAWAY' BOSS

MR JOHN IS a 'runaway' boss. He does not vanish forever; he will come back on sensing that the environment is conducive for his appearance. He tells his subordinates, 'Don't bring problems to me. Come with solutions.' Indeed it seems like a sensible approach. But is it really the empowerment of subordinates or simply an abdication of responsibilities? More often, it is the latter.

Bosses like John can shine only when the 'going is good'. The moment an issue or challenge comes up, they prefer to run away from the field. For example, they could postpone meetings if they fear that certain unpleasant issues will crop up. They might prefer to inspect field offices where they face lesser resistance. They might keep away from areas where troubleshooting and firm decisions are necessary, saying, 'I don't want any problems during my tenure.'

Runaway bosses also include those who would not run away literally, but never repond to proposals or requests. Due to their perennial lethargy or indecisiveness on important issues, they stack all the files for days, weeks and months. If you ask the status of your proposal or query, they would promptly say it is 'being examined' or 'under consideration'. However, this examination and consideration continues indefinitely.

The biggest challenge for a leader is not maintaining the status quo, but overseeing the changeover to a higher level of development. Runaway bosses do not like to be in the thick of action and their strategy is to train their subordinates not to allow anyone with problems to gain access to themselves. Over time, the staff often becomes adept in screening all the 'trouble-makers'. Only the problem-solvers and sycophants then have the ear of the boss!

Here is another characteristic: The boss cannot handle it if anyone contradicts his point of view. Instead of justifying his position or examining the contrary view, he would conclude the meeting abruptly. He simply 'runs away' from it.

An example of a runaway boss narrated by a manager in a software solution firm is very interesting: 'There was a client who visited our office with an unresolved issue. My boss told my team and me about the importance of the visit and subtly threatened us, saying "Don't goof up!" He also said, "Refer to me if the client is not happy with your explanation." However, when the client came, my boss made an excuse and left the office. That incident made me completely distrust him.'

Runaway bosses create runaway organizations!

Unfortunately, there are organizations that have to carry the load of a number of runaway bosses in the top management. Such organizations invariably become runaway organizations, as they would have to run away from clients, employees and other stakeholders due to a few bad bosses. A young civil servant shared this: 'There is an organization that is in the area of public service delivery. It is reluctant to organize any grievance redressal meetings. It is not only scared of the wrath of the public but also is conscious of its inability to provide any solution to or explanation of the problems.'

The omnipresent boss (except in the organization)

A CEO of a top IT Services company is fond of public appearances. He always likes to be with people outside the organization. All invitations to be a guest at cultural and social functions are accepted without any fuss or thought. He likes to be part of all panel discussions in the city and on television. However, his team leaders and other top managers of the organization rarely get a chance to meet him to discuss issues and get guidance. He gets worked up if someone approaches with a problem that requires immediate attention.

Though too much public engagement by CEOs takes away from their time being used for the organization's interests, Kotter and Mintzberg,[17] who are scholars and management experts, concluded that certain obligations to attend functions and ceremonies, though unimportant and time-wasters, can be advantageous for oneself and the organization. It is true that such public exposure can help the organization gain brand recognition. However, being absent from the workplace for too long should not become a way of shirking the real problems and grievances.

A successful leader is the one who never runs away from problems. Rather, he is one who considers every problem an opportunity to develop his and others' skills.

> **Are you a runaway boss?**
>
> Yes, if
> - ✓ You procrastinate on decisions
> - ✓ You do not like to face problems
> - ✓ You abdicate your responsibilities
> - ✓ You delegate more than required
> - ✓ You dislike listening to grievances
> - ✓ You are scared of being questioned by others
> - ✓ You like to absolve yourself from issues

Prescription for you, the boss

If you do not do what you are supposed to, someone else will (and soon sit on your seat).

The more you procrastinate on a decision, the more problematic it will become to decide.

If you run away from a battle, you might fall into a much tougher and longer battle.

Precaution for you

Try and communicate your concerns to your boss without being aggressive or trying to show him in poor light. However, escalate the matter if it starts affecting your work too much.

Precept for the organization

Organizations need to formulate timeframes for decisions even at the highest level, as well as put in place a prompt reporting system that confirms everyone's accountability.

The signs of recovery

A true leader is at the immediate reach of the team whenever they face a challenge. He has the confidence to find a remedy to any problem, especially when the team has attempted and failed.

4

MR BOSS, YOU ARE PETTY!

'OH MAN, HE is so petty!', 'How could he stoop so low while holding such a senior position?' are oft-repeated comments one hears from team members about their bosses. People believe that as professionals climb higher in the hierarchy, they become more magnanimous and generous. It beats them when they see bosses behaving like one of them or even more pettily.

When someone perceives a boss as petty, what does he mean? The question was put to middle-level managers from private and public sectors and they were asked to respond with instances of pettiness.

The responses were revealing:

a) When the boss pokes his nose in an area or situation that has to be left to his subordinates
b) When he does not offer seats to the subordinates when they meet him
c) When he denies leave requested for a genuine need
d) When he makes cryptic remarks in meetings
e) When he brags that he gained a good deal by bargaining hard with a street vendor
f) When he expects his subordinates to do personal work for him and refuses to compensate for the same
g) When he nominates himself for an assignment or training primarily designed for his subordinates
h) When he expects his subordinates to pay for his personal expenses
i) When he penalizes a team member for a minor omission when he himself makes similar mistakes
j) When he makes disparaging comments about his colleagues to his subordinates
k) When he reprimands very senior employees in front of their subordinates
l) When he fixes a review meeting for all managers in an inconvenient remote station because he has personal work to attend to there

Are people aware that they are being seen as petty by others? Some are and some are not. Further, those who are aware fall into two categories. The first is where the individual justifies his pettiness as he thinks he has every right to be like that and his behaviour was appropriate at the time. The second type is where the individual knows that he is petty, but despairs about his inability to discard the habit. Finally, there are others who wallow in pettiness but are blissfully ignorant of it.

What is the cause of pettiness? For some, it is a personality trait, but for many others, the pettiness of others has rubbed off on them. There are bosses who change colour according to the behaviour pattern of their own bosses. If the seniors are petty, they often out-do them in pettiness. Who knows, if they have a generous boss they might become paragons of that virtue after a while!

Mrs Roy, a senior director in a large organization, loved Chinese cuisine, and desired the same at work parties. All the heads of divisions under her had to scout for the best Chinese restaurants in town, and ensure that it was always a fresh experience for her. It was whispered that those who didn't manage to do this got a poor appraisal.

Some senior executives in a defence organization in India commented, 'We had to bring expensive birthday gifts for our bosses on many occasions in a year: both on the official and *desi* birthdays of the boss and his wife, and one each for Diwali, New Year and their wedding anniversary. In fact, some of us forget our wives' birthdays and our own wedding anniversaries, but not the boss's and his wife's.'

Grover was fond of travel and used to make frequent visits to his field offices. As he worked in a large insurance company with offices in most towns, he expected the staff at each location to take care of his breaks for lunch, coffee and dinner at the most expensive joints. If he travelled by train, the staff needed to visit him at each railway station with food, fruits and sweets. When he travelled by air, if his staff had not got him a seat in the front row, he would become really furious. If he stayed at a guest house he expected to be allotted the best room there!

Robert, the vice-president of a large manufacturing firm, is fed up of his boss not for his expectation to achieve targets, but for the expectation of front row tickets for every fashion show or celebrity and cultural programme in the city. 'It is easy when our company is a sponsor of these programmes or the function is organized by our partners. But even in other cases, he expects his team to spend money to get him tickets. Whenever I cannot do so, his immediate response is that I'm not resourceful enough. Unfortunately, this also reflects in his attitude and behaviour towards me at work.'

Bosses like those referred to above consider it their right to avail of services from subordinates to fulfil personal needs. Such practices create a culture of dishonesty and frustration, which ultimately leads to unfairness in decision-making.

An ideal leader should be broad in his outlook, magnanimous in his responses and refined in his behaviour.

Prescription for you, the boss

Don't let the credibility you might have built through sincere work or big achievements shrink because of petty behaviour. For a little gain, don't spoil your chance to be labelled as a positive role model.

Precaution for you

You could insulate your boss from generating an adverse public image on account of his pettiness through your intelligent interventions, but being party to his pettiness as a matter of practice would result in you being branded petty as well.

Precept for the organization

Organizations cannot possibly monitor and act against all petty behaviour by bosses. However, they could definitely identify such individuals based on feedback and make firm 'people decisions' about those who indulge in continued pettiness that can ultimately affect the image of the organization.

The signs of recovery

When petty bosses and behaviour disappear, the organization will be respected for its decency, magnanimity and honesty.

5

WHEN THE BOSS IS A 'SNOOPERVISER'

HERE IS MR Mittal. He is second in line after the CEO. He is in charge of all acquisitions, is quite an efficient man and a workaholic too. But his team members are not happy with him, mainly due to his suspicious nature. He snoops on their mails, checks what time the team members come and go indirectly through personal staff, and keeps tabs on their visitors. He even enters their cabins when they are not present.

Paranoid or suspicious bosses such as this one perceive hidden motives in others' actions and believe that people are out to cheat them. They create feelings of insecurity and claustrophobia within an organization. If a team head does not trust his members, it can result in lack of commitment and poor performance.

People hate 'snoopervisers'!

Shaw was the chief officer of a law enforcement agency. He was a very efficient and honest man. However, most officers did not want to work under him. Whenever someone was posted under him, there would be an outpouring of sympathy for that individual. This is because Shaw was known for snooping on his investigation team to check if they were honest. Though he was a very senior officer who did not need to be in the field, he would do so out of sheer suspicion of junior officers. Due to this behaviour, even efficient and responsible officials disliked his presence.

There is an anonymous quote: 'Some people will believe anything if it's whispered to them'. Snoopervisers are like that; they tend to collect feedback about one team member from another. They call each member separately to get details of the activities of the others. When members find out that their boss does not trust them and even snoops on their activities, they lose morale, are dissatisfied and have no enthusiasm to do their best. It was Abraham Maslow who emphasized that individuals prefer fulfilment of 'esteem needs' (a sense of accomplishment) and that 'self-actualization' is preferred by individuals over physiological and safety needs. Trust is an important attribute for the well-being of individuals in any organization. Self-determination theorists have argued that fulfilment of certain basic psychological needs such as autonomy and relatedness are required for overall well-being.[18]

Trust needs to be mutual

Trust begets trust. Unless you trust the other person, you can't expect that person to trust you. In fact, some believe you don't deserve trust from the other if you are suspicious of them.

There was a senior vice-president of a large multinational company based in San Francisco who was posted to a South Asian city. Before this, he had not had a housekeeper to look after his domestic affairs. Thus, in his new house he was always suspicious of the maid and thought she would cheat him by stealing money or goods from him. He had an idea for finding out if she was: in the first week of appointing the lady, he kept a currency note on a side table before leaving for office. It was basically a test for the maid: if she was honest, the money would stay where it was. Though he found the notes at the same place even after two days, he wanted to make doubly sure that the maid was honest. So the next time, he left his wallet on the dining table. The maid obviously understood the frantic 'assessments' of her suspicious employer, and left him without even taking the salary for the days she worked.

'Great place to work' has conducted research for over 25 years to identify great workplaces around the world. It says, 'Managers who trust their employees allow innovative ideas to come up from all levels of the company. Employees who trust each other report a sense of camaraderie and feeling of being part of a family. Together they deliver far more than the sum of their individual efforts.'[19]

℞ Prescription for you, the boss

Understand that chronic suspicion is a disease that causes negativity all around. The only antidote is to consciously start trusting people around you. Avoid indulging in micro management. By giving them sufficient freedom to be creative in work, you nurture competency in them and in turn develop the competency of the organization.

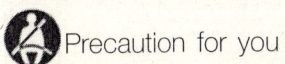
Precaution for you

While accusing the boss of being a suspicious person, it is also necessary to look at yourself and figure out if you are really honest and committed in your work. You need to demonstrate your credibility before the boss.

You should regularly meet and discuss work with such individuals to help them trust you as a team member. Further, be careful when you say anything about your boss to others, since they might keep tabs on members. Understanding his priorities, frank communication at every opportunity, seeking his advice at various stages, and other positive steps can make relationships with suspicious bosses a little smoother.

Precept for the organization

The more suspicious bosses there are in an organization, the more trust-deficient the organization becomes. The culture of mistrust can spread in and form a set pattern that influences internal procedures related to vigilance, inspection, appraisal and 'hire and fire'.

It is impossible for organizations to check whether a person suffers from chronic suspicion at the time of recruitment. However, assessing and managing such individuals internally can help ensure that their behaviour does not negatively affect the performance of the team. Overall, only by creating a culture of frank communication along with avenues for confidential feedback can organizations identify people who repose trust in others and also gain trust from them.

The signs of recovery

In an environment of mutual trust, both the boss and the team can expect respect, behavioural integrity, commitment and excellence from each other.

Author in conversation with S.D. Shibulal

Tackling the trust deficit in the organizations

What are the possible causes of lack of trust within organizations?
There are multiple reasons for the lack of trust perceived in organizations. I would like to enumerate three major reasons. First is the leadership style in the organization. If the leader prefers a 'divide and rule' policy, mistrust is bound to be present. Top executives have to set the right tone for good leadership in order to create an environment of trust. The second factor is the precipitation of

people-based conflicts more than issue-based ones. The third reason is over-ambition of some individuals that is not in tune with the long-term interests of the organization. Ambition is good to have and must be encouraged. However, blind overambition could be counter-productive and might impact the environment of trust within the organization.

What are the consequences of the perception of a trust deficit within the organization?
Organizations are dynamic entities where there is a constant interplay of people and processes from within and outside. Every interaction and transaction is guided by certain practices, procedures and expectations. In an environment of mistrust, the costs for completing a task successfully increases. This is not just monetary loss; valuable time is also lost in managing conflicts and misunderstandings. When there is lack of trust, there is difficulty in identifying the real issue and resolving the same.

How can an exemplary leader build trust in the organization/ team he is leading?
If you don't trust people, none of them will trust you. You need to lead by example as well as be fair and transparent. Leaders should not only trust their team but also explicitly communicate the same for clarity. They should have a management style that ensures cohesion rather than conflict within the managerial team. Finally, they should appreciate exemplary work and reward people with the correct values.

Can you give an example of this from your corporate experience?
I've found that 360-degree evaluation is an effective tool in understanding the issues, attitudes and perceptions of people comprehensively. The challenge of the 360-degree evaluation is that it is very private. Many years ago, when I was in charge of a group, to create a culture of mutual trust and to build the team, I used this tool. We did a mutual evaluation within the core members. Normally

this is done confidentially; however, I suggested that we sit together and analyse the results. Each one of us shared our feedback and gave responses on whether the feedback was perceived as correct and fair. As the leader, I took the initiative to share the feedback I got, my views on the same and the steps I would take to improve based on the inputs received. People were very apprehensive initially, since it would expose them in front of others. Those who were very frank and forthcoming in sharing their feedback were the ones who were determined to take corrective action. Those who were reluctant to share the feedback were the ones who got the least benefit from the exercise. Within a couple of years, the system got institutionalized in the organization. To me, this was an instance of demonstration of trust and an exercise in learning how to trust others.

What are your other suggestions in order to create an environment of trust and well-being within the organization?
Some vital steps that any organization can take:

a. To start open evaluation, feedback sharing, and discussion on corrective action within the team, so that one can definitely see trust nurturing in those organizations.
b. An innovative performance management system that is fair and transparent must be established.
c. Well-formulated and meticulously executed team-building workshops can take place. (Many times, certain tough decisions can be taken in relaxed environments where people understand the rationale of the decisions and accept them. There will be more constructive feedback in such settings).
d. Frequent off-site interaction programs
e. Outings with families
f. Having periodic group calls rather than only one-on-one calls.
g. Training on ethical leadership is necessary for young managers. Every new manager should know that there is no alternative to fairness, transparency and honesty. They should be taught not

just principles and practices, but also the techniques to be used. They should be familiarized with time-tested and successful techniques such as unique performance management tools, balance score card, 360-degree evaluation, conflict resolution strategies and communication enhancement skills.

h. There are many large corporations where the senior management team has contributed, worked to build step by step and stayed together for a long time before expanding to new horizons. People need to put aside their differences and personal aspirations and work towards the common cause. That is where performance, progress and success can happen. A leader who can make this happen can create miracles.

S.D. Shibulal is the co-founder, former member of the Board, CEO and MD of Infosys. He, along with others, is giving shape to a global business incubator to help entrepreneurs and early-stage firms succeed in diverse verticals.

6

THE TIME BANDITS

TIME IS AN extremely valuable resource for any company. You can judge an organization by closely examining how its employees utilize their time. How an individual spends his time at work is very important to assess the work culture and overall results. Of course, that doesn't mean one is expected to work incessantly like a machine; everyone needs time to relax and rejuvenate during work hours.

What if the boss eats into the team's time?

The success of bosses lies in delegating. The oldest and the crudest definition of management is that it is the art of getting things done. That means the people whom bosses delegate to should be able to deliver their best within a specific time schedule. Most organizations plan their requirements and give necessary resources to execute them. However, one thing that often does not get factored in is the time the bosses themselves take from their team members while the latter are on projects.

Thus, even if projects and schedules are cleared and relevant resources are available for delivery, if the members in the team are given additional responsibilities by the boss, it can affect the team's morale and efficiency. Unfortunately, such additional tasks or responsibilities cannot be disregarded or resented, often being inevitable in upholding the interest of the organization.

Further, every task or project contains a series of steps that need to be completed at an appropriate time. Often, however, though the execution is delegated, the design can contain vetting or clearance by bosses at various stages. Even when the team does an excellent job and completes each stage ahead of the time schedule, a lethargic or unsystematic boss can hold his approval, delaying the project and creating unreasonable pressure on the team.

The worst situation is when the team is headed by a boss who is nothing but a 'time bandit'. He is the one who calls you for silly reasons and keeps you engaged with unwanted advice, worthless narrations or unnecessary probing. Another boss might affectionately invite you for a cup of tea when you are neck-deep in work. It might be relaxing in a way but can lead to a prolonged conversation if the boss is in an expansive mood. He does not realizes that the other person has to be at his desk to complete the task on hand. Further, many bosses need gossip-mongers. By virtue of their solitary position, they rarely get news of whatever is happening within the organization: who is doing what, information on fresh affairs, new cliques, idiosyncrasies of predecessors and other bosses, family issues of employees, views of people about themselves, and so on. While bosses do need to know their environment and its people, a line has to be drawn somewhere on gossip. Famous management consultant and author Peter Drucker[20] has said, 'Time is the scarcest resource, and unless it is managed, nothing else can be managed.'

Social networking or social not-working?

In a study[21] reported in the *Journal of Medical Internet Research*, it was found that staff at the critical care division in hospitals spent about 20 per cent of their time on Facebook; surprisingly, their Facebook usage increased with the increase in patient volume and severity of work. Though the study ultimately concluded that these time-outs led to improved worker functioning, it also stated that it might have compromised the quality of patient care. In another study[22] authorized by Microsoft on social networking crossing boundaries, it was found that though better networking increased productivity, it also contributed to tensions that occurred from transgressing hierarchy, status and power boundaries.

The time spent by and the extent of involvement of bosses on social networking sites can also adversely influence the behaviour of team members in different ways. The following are some possible scenarios: a) when the team member sees that the boss is online during working hours, b) when the employee sends a friend request to the boss on the networking site, c) when the boss sends or accepts a friend request from the employee, and d) when the team members start commenting or liking the boss's posts or vice versa. Unless there is self-restraint or discipline maintained in the online interactions between the boss and the team members, there is every possibility of tensions, strains, misinterpretation and communication gaps springing up and affecting relationships that are primarily built on hierarchy, status and power boundaries.

CISCO has released a tool along with a detailed solution guide for enterprises on controlling Facebook activities at work. Additionally, some of the larger companies have created internal avenues for relaxation by offering radio and web broadcasts. Infosys, for example, has a system in their Bangalore (Bengaluru) campus where employees can listen to their favourite music through a customized broadcasting network within the organization. SAS, one of the companies shortlisted by *Fortune* Magazine and its partners as the best company to work at, launched its first ever internal social media network called The Hub as early as 2011. More than 5800 employees registered on it within the first 60 days, demonstrating the yearning of people to have a vent at work.

Diagnose the disease yourself

John works in an organization that is suffering from mismanagement due to procrastination by and inefficiency of certain key managers in the head office. Kim, a senior manager, finally replied to the repeated calls made by John, a junior officer, seeking the status of an urgent proposal sent for approval. Kim explained to John how much the work pressure was mounting at headquarters, narrating the inefficiencies of some staff, how he tried to deal with certain crises and how pressing matters were not getting cleared on time. He also shared his achievements in the organizations he had worked in

> earlier along with his attempts to improve the system. He spoke for about half an hour, abruptly ending the conversation on receiving another call. Nothing could be discussed about the status of the proposal sent by John.
>
> Have you found out the cause of the disease in the above organization? What is your prescription for the work environment there?

Prescription for you, the boss

If you use your time at work efficiently, responsibly and meaningfully, your team members will follow suit. Otherwise, you cannot expect them to be effective time managers.

You do not have the right to reprimand a time bandit team member if you do not judiciously use your time at work.

Precaution for you

If you have a time bandit boss, take him out of your 'role models' list immediately. If you are tempted to take advantage of his laxity and overindulge in social networking platforms or gossiping, be aware that you could kill your creativity and lose your drive to excel at work.

Precept for the organization

Establishing a secured private network or blocking certain networking sites would not serve the purpose as people can still get access to these through personal smart devices. Create a policy that restricts the usage of social networking sites by everyone, from the top boss to the junior-most team member. However, ensure that it does not affect the morale of the team. A proper policy can be formulated after consulting the representatives of the employees.

The signs of recovery

A well-managed organization values time, creates disciplined time budgets and conducts regular time audits.

7

THE TOWERING BOSSES

MR MENON IS one of the senior directors in an organization. Though he is in charge of Human Resource Management, his subordinates say that he seems to be one of the most inhuman officers. Menon has given strict instructions to everyone that nobody is allowed to meet him without a prior appointment through his secretary. Further, the secretary has been told to deny appointments in the first instance. Only if people persist and beg for a meeting will they be given a slot, which is also not immediate. He basically wants people to believe that he is very busy and does not wish to encourage walk-in visitors.

One division head, who had recently joined the organization, faced a serious HR issue within his division and wanted to personally meet the managing director to brief him. As he used to in his previous organization, he called up the managing director—who is just one level above him—and requested a meeting. The managing director got annoyed and said, 'Contact my secretary if you want to get a meeting fixed with me.' The response was shocking for the senior manager. He told his colleague, 'This is the first time in my 15 years of working that I have been so rudely treated by a boss. I don't think I will be able to work under such bosses.' After joining the new organization with a lot of motivation and eagerness to bring in innovations, the division head felt disappointed and almost felt like quitting.

Unapproachable bosses tend to keep a distance from their subordinates and often fail to understand the people around them. They wear the garb of a 'serious' taskmaster. Their juniors might fear them and hold back on giving them any honest feedback. There can also be overall dissatisfaction in their teams.

We are used to hearing this phrase: 'Content is the king; conversation is the queen'. Boris Groysberg and Michael Slind say that leadership is a conversation.[23] They conducted a research project on the state of organizational communication in the 21st century and found that smart leaders engage with employees in a way that resembles an ordinary 'person-to-person' conversation, rather than through one-sided commands. They identified four elements of organizational conversation that reflect the key attributes of interpersonal conversation: intimacy, interactivity, inclusion and intentionality.

Robert Greene, in his 16th Law of power,[24] advises that if you 'make yourself too available then the aura of power you have created around yourself will wear away. Turn the game around: make yourself less accessible and you increase the value of your presence.' However, in the post-globalized world where changes happen rapidly, decisions need to be taken every moment and the team needs to be motivated and directed to new areas for the survival of the organization, no leader can afford to play the game of hide and seek. Thus, an absence like this would not create respect and esteem. Richard Boyatzis and Annie McKee wrote:[25] 'Mindfulness, hope and compassion are the three key elements for resonant leadership.' Being present and being respected is the new ball game. The belief that 'familiarity breeds contempt' is passé.

The need for a zero hour

Under the rules of proceedings of the Indian Parliament, there is a provision called Zero Hour. This is a period when any Member of Parliament can ask a question concerning administration, governance or issues of public interest by giving notice prior to the start of daily proceedings to the Speaker/Chairman. Similarly, it is necessary for bosses of large organizations to give time to team members to meet them and discuss or share issues. Caroline Ghosn, CEO, the Levo League said:[26] 'Dedicate one hour a week to hosting office hours: open your door, block your calendar and invite your team to drop in and share.'

Here is an example of a senior officer at a large public organization of about 10,000 officers and 50,000 staff who holds the most important position with highly sensitive and demanding tasks. She is responsible for reporting to the highest functionaries in the government, including a cabinet minister. Every minute of hers is valuable. She hardly gets time at home because of the pressure of official tasks. However, the first thing she did as soon as she was elevated to the post was to send out a letter across the organization, welcoming anyone with an unsettled grievance to meet her or send their messages or grievances at an exclusive email id monitored by her personally. She strongly believes that every official is an asset and the output and overall success of the organization depends on their happiness.

Unapproachable boss is a 'loser'

An unapproachable boss doesn't earn the respect of people around him. He does not get real feedback about the organization as he fails to be receptive to people. Thus, the ultimate loser is the organization itself. It is imperative that those with excellent communication and management skills are the ones who are appointed to the top levels in any organization. Training in soft skills is also as important at the top levels as in the lower ones. Though there may be criticism that it is wasteful to 'apply manure at the fag end', it is necessary to do so in many organizations, especially those where top leadership positions are filled up solely on the basis of seniority.

When the real boss called!

'I don't want any callers this afternoon,' said the boss to his secretary, 'And if they say that their business is important, just tell them that everyone says the same thing.'

That afternoon his wife called and insisted on seeing him. When the secretary refused, she said, 'I am his wife,' to which the secretary replied, 'That's what they all say.'

(Ramani and Varma)[27]

(Of course, this happened when there were no cellphones!)

Step out of the tower

1. Develop a keen interest in knowing about the employees

The boss needs to have an understanding of the backgrounds of his team members. If the span of control is large, the boss should have ready access to each employee's profile, which contains family details, leave history, relevant medical history, recent career profile, and other information.

2. Receptivity
The attitude, temperament, behaviour and visible expressions of the boss should be such that no one would hesitate to approach him with an issue.

3. Enthusiasm
No one likes a boss who is lethargic, sluggish and too matter of fact. Bosses should have the ability to make the other person comfortable and forthcoming with ideas and opinions. His overall body language should be oriented towards those who come to converse with him. Who would like to interact with a person who has a disinterested air about him?

4. Availability
The boss should be mobile. That doesn't mean that he should not spend time in his cabin; but he should be available for people to see him with regularity. If he is frequently away on travel or spends most of his time only with his boss or colleagues, it would affect smooth upward communication.

8

WORKING WITH 'HYPER-INTELLIGENT' BOSSES

A BOSS WHO is exceptionally brilliant in conceptualization, planning and implementation would be a boon for any organization. However, when intelligence is combined with obstinacy or rigidity, it can turn counter-productive.

Hussain leads about 400 managers in his company. He believes that his intellectual acuity is higher than that of everyone else at his level and below him. He believes only in top-down approaches and does not encourage suggestions from juniors. He justifies his actions by stating that whatever he does is in the best interest of the organization.

If the sole aim of bosses like Hussain is to maximize benefits for the organization without focusing on the development and

welfare of the people, they will most certainly face resentment from their teams, who would regard them as too self-absorbed or manipulative.

It is written in *Tao Te Ching* that:
'It is hard to lead
When we try to be too clever.
Too much cleverness undermines group harmony.
Those who lead without such strategies
Bring blessing to all.'[28]

N.R. Narayana Murthy, chief mentor and one of the founders of Infosys, wrote the following in a letter to shareholders:

'Many intelligent people possess a high ego and low patience to deal with people less capable than themselves. Leaders have to manage this anomaly very carefully, counsel these errant people from time to time, and allow them to operate as long as they do not become dysfunctional and start harming the organization. If they do cross the threshold, it takes courage to inform the individuals that their time in the organization is over and that they have to leave.'[29]

Andrew Campbell and two other scholars[30] analysed the question 'Why do good leaders make bad decisions?'. They argued that important decisions made by intelligent, responsible people with the best information and intentions are sometimes hopelessly flawed. They found that leaders could be affected by three factors or biases: a) the presence of inappropriate self-interest, b) the presence of distorting attachments, and c) the presence of misleading memories.

Hyper-intelligent leaders have the tendency to stick to their own judgements even when they are presented with a different view. Some are uncompromising in their beliefs and positions and are guided solely by their own experiences. They are adamant in their views and not willing to change. They tend to justify themselves when mistakes or negative fallouts are pointed out. Even when it is ultimately proved from the outcome that they were wrong, such individuals try to find some reason to attribute the failure to other factors.

The reason for the above can be a feeling of superiority based on an excessive estimation of one's intelligence, coupled with an underestimation of the intelligence of people around. Due to this, some hyper-intelligent bosses may also tend to ridicule, intimidate or ignore others.

Further, there are bosses who take credit depending on the outcome of a particular action. They attribute their involvement for the success of a task or project. When the action results in failure, however, they might say 'I had warned that it would be a failure.' Rosabeth Moss Kanter,[31] the author of the book *Confidence,* called such behaviour the 'timidity of mediocrity'.

If team members feel that their boss will not listen to them even if they try to convince him, what about colleagues, advisers or the bosses of the boss? Does the boss listen to them? E. Kelly et al. have found in a study[32] that as power increases, the tendency to take advice decreases, even when the advice can help people perform better or make better decisions. This phenomenon of egocentric discounting of advice is also highlighted by L. Yaniv.[33] Bill Gates said: 'Fear should guide you. I consider failure on a regular basis.'

Omniscient bosses are not assets, but liabilities for organizations that aim to nurture young leaders for better prospects, for themselves as well as the organization.

℞ Prescription for you, the boss

It is important to understand that intelligence has nothing to do with one's position in the hierarchy. Often, inputs from people you rate as 'less intelligent' can lead to better output. A truly intelligent leader identifies, appreciates and taps the perceptiveness and intuitiveness of people around him.

Precaution for you

Don't feel intimidated by a hyper-intelligent boss. No one can claim that he is omniscient. You must not lose confidence due to the indifference and rejection of overconfident bosses. Instead, continue to contribute your best irrespective of their behaviour or lack of recognition.

Precept for the organization

Organizations should establish practices that promote creative ideas and suggestions from everyone, including juniors. This kind of collective wisdom is far superior to the thinking of a single obstinate individual.

The signs of recovery

In an era where crowdsourcing is popular, a leader who accepts and acknowledges the views and creativity of the team will be respected for his social intelligence and sensitivity.

9

THE FAULT-FINDERS

NO ONE CAN deny that bosses have the right to point out their juniors' faults at work. However, what if that is the only work the boss does, and that too with a lot of biases?

There are several chronic fault-finders in our midst. Giving honest feedback to others on their contributions is constructive; it can facilitate correction and improvement. However, if there is only fault-finding based on personal perceptions and attitudes rather than through an objective analysis of facts and expectations, it can be destructive and demotivating for the recipient. One needs to look at others and their actions in terms of what they are capable of under given circumstances and resources.

Often, fault-finders expect others to think and act the way they do without appreciating the fact that no two personalities are alike. Such bosses are intimidating, ineffective leaders. People usually desist from interacting with such cynical 'know-all' types of leaders.

A young manager had this to share: 'Whenever I started sharing a new idea with my boss, the first word with which he interrupted my talk was "No". Then he would continue justifying this for the next half an hour without even allowing me to complete.' Another employee said: 'If I go with a proposal to my boss, even before he starts reading, he opens his red-inked pen to correct what I have written. This particular act irritates me, since he assumes there would definitely be some mistakes to be corrected. He misses the actual idea because he is too preoccupied with the nuances of language.'

Fault-finders are of three types. First are those who are perfectionists. They maintain certain standards and want others to do the same. The second category are those who are not perfectionists themselves, but they want the team to achieve perfection according to the standards set by others. They themselves would commit the same faults they point out in the work of the team, but they don't tolerate any shortcomings and want the team to achieve perfection. The third category includes the ones who are neither perfectionist themselves nor interested in meeting the expectations or standards of others. They want to find fault just for the sake of it. They consider it their duty to find faults and they have a whale of a time doing that!

For he knows not what he does...

John was a successful CEO who received many awards for his innovations in the organization. That prompted me to interview him, in order to understand his successful leadership styles. During our chat, he explained how he has led his team to achieve outstanding results. He narrated his working style: he reaches much before the normal office time and stays late every day. He holds frequent meetings with each project team and evaluates the progress of work on a regular basis. For certain important projects, he holds review meetings every day. He corrects the mistakes of the team and gives his inputs at every stage. He believes that his personal intervention has improved the quality of the output.

After meeting John, I met his project teams separately. Each one of them said they felt tortured by their boss; he interfered in their work regularly, picking up trivial issues and engaging in unending discussions. Because of this they had to resort to unnecessary deviations in the project plan that resulted in more cost and time input without any concrete results. Above all, they felt 'inferior' because of the constant nagging by the boss in front of the other team leaders and felt suffocated because of the unnecessary control, which deprived them of independence in making decisions. They simply could not stand their boss for breathing down their necks.

The above illustration shows how the actions of a fault-finder boss are perceived by his team members. Unfortunately, many bosses are under the illusion that they have done a marvellous job, little realizing the disdain teams may have for them. Such bosses are also prone to think that they are instrumental in bringing out perfection in the work. However, according to Paul Hewitt,[34] a practising psychologist and professor at the University of British Columbia, the zeal for perfection has a direct relation to depression, anxiety, eating disorders, and mental health problems.

A young woman told her neighbour: 'My husband is employed by a large corporation as an efficiency expert.' When the neighbour asked what an efficiency expert does, the woman replied, 'Well when we, the wives, do it, they call it nagging'![35]

Why do they hate to appreciate others?

Much has been written on the positive influence of appreciation and praise on the motivation and performance levels of people. Even then, some of the most highly trained managers from top business schools are very miserly when it comes to praising others. Some bosses think that if they praise someone for their good work, the person would get 'too big for their boots' and would not bother to improve further. Others think that the more faults they detect, the more improvement there is in performance. In the article 'Connect, then lead', Amy Cuddy, Matthew Kohut and John Neffinger[36] stated that a leader should be like a Happy Warrior. They said, 'If you show your employees that you hold roughly the same worldview they do, you demonstrate not only empathy but, in their eyes, common sense—the ultimate qualification for being listened to.'

Chronic fault-finders not only demotivate the team but also harm the reputation of its members. A friend said to me, 'My boss is well suited as a speaker for funerals. The only time I see him showering appreciation on any employee is when he leaves the job.'

Prescription for you, the boss

Practise accepting occasional imperfections from the team. Understand that no individual is perfect and that absolute perfection is a myth.

Precaution for you

Don't take the faults pointed out by bosses personally. If your boss is known to be a 'fault-finder', understand that being patient is better than being angry.

Precept for the organization

Identify chronic fault-finders and make them understand how their approach is counter-productive. They should also be made aware of the costs incurred because of frequent interference in projects and activities.

Unreformed fault-finders should not be involved in crucial projects since their style of work can reduce innovation and creativity, and their over-supervision can put a spoke in the organization's wheel.

An environment that is conducive to exchanging proper feedback within the organization should be created, so that it can reduce the strains resulting from fault-finding.

The signs of recovery

The right leaders appreciate good points in the team and recognize the wrongs as a need for further support, development and encouragement.

10

MR BOSS, ARE YOU OUT OF YOUR MIND?!

COMING OUT OF the chamber of the boss, Mr Joe shouted to his colleagues, 'He is eccentric. The other day, he was very supportive of my project idea. And now he behaves as if my idea is nonsense.' Others agreed that the boss's behaviour was unpredictable. One day he was most gentle and placid and another day he would be rough, perturbed and fuming.

Behavioural and temperamental inconsistencies of individuals who occupy important positions can certainly affect the organization negatively. Occasional mood swings are natural and acceptable, but no one likes an individual with an erratic personality.

Nair was a boss who used to behave badly during his spells of emotional upheaval. Fortunately for the people around him, his personal staff worked well as an insulator. They prevented others from entering his chamber unless it was for an emergency, and would intimate the team as soon as Nair got back to his normal self. One day, an officer who had worked under him during his good old years came to meet him. The personnel prevented him from going in, stating that he was reprimanding a counsel as he was upset over certain remarks related to one of the cases of the organization before the High Court. The officer brushed aside the objection and went inside confidently to meet his old boss. The moment he entered the chamber, he was hit on the face by a bunch of files thrown by the boss, who was terribly angry at the counsel sitting there!

In a cricket match organized by the officers' club, a young officer amazed people by his exceptional 'catches'. People asked him for the secret of this skill. He said, 'I have a boss who is in the habit of throwing pen-drives at us if he gets data or reports that are not to his liking. That's how I became adept at catching!'

Most organizations have extensive screening processes to select the most appropriate person for the job. They employ various tests to check the competence of the candidate in the area of language skills, technical skills, reasoning ability, comprehension skills, job aptitude, and so on. However, very few organizations employ proper tests to check a candidate's emotional quotient, social quotient, or overall competence to deal with colleagues, subordinates, superiors and other people. A successful person is the one who can keep his emotions under control. While it is justifiable to show emotion in certain situations, if one continues to express anger, depression, or unhappiness to another unrelated person or in an unrelated circumstance or environment, then that is not acceptable behaviour. Researchers Paul Babiak and Robert Hare[37] have found that one out of 25 corporate bosses is a psychopath. Though they enter as rising stars and corporate saviours, all too soon they start abusing the trust of colleagues and manipulating promoters or supervisors.

People are often branded 'moody' because of their frequent spells of negative emotion or prolonged 'executive angst'. Others wait for the days when they are in a good mood in order to interact with them. Such people may not be suited to the leadership roles in an organization.

Emotional maturity

Jeff Kehoe,[38] after analysing a few books written about political heads, namely, Thomas Jefferson, Abraham Lincoln and Lyndon Johnson, arrived at the conclusion that in politics and business, effective leadership requires, more than the right skills and strategies, an acceptable personality type. The most important ingredient of a rounded personality is emotional maturity. Goleman and others[39] found in a study that the more senior the leader, the more important emotional competency becomes.

Can a person develop emotional maturity later in life, especially if his younger period was dotted with emotional outbursts and unpredictable moods? Are these behavioural patterns created by nature or nurture? Though many researchers tend to attribute these traits to one's genes, a few studies give hope to those who would like to change. LeDoux's research[40] points towards this. Also, Davidson and others,[41] in their work from the perspective of neuroscience, titled 'Emotion, Plasticity, Context and Regulation' have argued that the brain circuitry of emotion exhibits a fair degree of plasticity.

℞ Prescription for you, the boss

Don't expect everyone in your team to dance to your moods. No one appreciates a moody boss. Keep your emotions within boundaries.

Precaution for you

Have the wisdom to maintain a distance while your boss is moody. Gauge his emotional status before approaching him with an important problem or plan.

Don't react to a moody boss; instead, withdraw strategically. Discretion is the better part of valour!

Precept for the organization

The Emotional Quotient of a person should be a crucial criterion when deciding on promoting him to a leadership position. Some are innately emotionally less developed while some might become more mature as they go forward. Therefore, organizations need to be on a continuous or regular evaluation mode, especially when people are due for elevation.

The signs of recovery

When bosses stop displaying their moods in the organization, people start respecting them for their emotional maturity. This would definitely result in stability and consistency at all levels in the organization.

Why did they hate their bosses?

Even a single incident can make people dislike their bosses. See some examples shared by the interviewees.
- I was denied a day's leave to attend the funeral of my aunt who brought me up while I was a child. The boss couldn't understand my bond with that aunt. He insisted that I find a colleague to cover my shift on that day. I couldn't find anyone and he refused the leave, stating, 'Anyway she was not your mother!'
- He dismissed my unique business idea as silly. Later I was astonished to find that he presented the same idea to his bosses as his own and got accolades. He didn't have the courtesy to

- acknowledge my effort even in private.
- He shouted at me in the presence of several colleagues and subordinates in a meeting even after I explained that the delay was not attributable to me.
- I got approval for going on a holiday two months in advance and booked tickets for the family and made all arrangements. But my boss cancelled my leave just two days before the date of departure, ignoring my promise that I would complete all urgent work before going on holiday.
- I had to leave my job because of my boss. He was a software start-up guy trying to develop an interesting online media portal. He was young and didn't have training in media or humanities, and had no prior experience with employees. He believed that he was empowering women employees by asking them to work 24×7 like his single software guys. Women who were married and had responsibilities felt stressed by his demands. I stood up for them as a senior manager. He was furious and his software mates were incredibly insulting to me. I was forced to leave. The whole experience left me traumatized.

As a boss, what is your takeaway from the above?

Why did they like their bosses?

We have seen earlier how even a single incident can make people dislike their bosses. See some examples of how a single good gesture could make people like their bosses.
- When I committed a mistake, my boss called me and said, 'Mistakes do happen, just forget about it, and go ahead with the work.'
- When I suggested a new project, my boss encouraged me and said, 'Don't be apprehensive about the results. You have my full support. Just go ahead with your experiments.'
- When I made some small progress in my work, my boss said, 'We

should celebrate this success.' That was very motivating.
- When we were struggling with a problem in the software project, my boss stayed back and rolled up his sleeves and found an elegant solution to the problem. If that was not inspirational enough, in the presentation before his boss he gave full credit to us for the breakthrough. And not a whisper about his effort!
- When I had committed a blunder out of sheer negligence, my boss defended me before his boss.
- When a bomb blast occurred in our city, the boss telephoned all the employees and enquired about their well-being.
- When my boss rescheduled my work to enable me to take care of my sick child even though there was an urgent client delivery.
- When my father was diagnosed with cancer, my boss gave me a transfer to my hometown, on compassionate grounds, on the very same day of my making the request!
- When he gave me a complimentary ticket for the 'Club Class' of the cricket match and said, 'You are really burned out with work. Take your family tomorrow to watch the cricket match.'

As a boss, do you think some of the above team members are yours too?

11

WHO WILL BELL THE BOSS?

THE STORY OF the emperor's new clothes by Hans Christian Andersen is well-known—a young boy had the audacity to cry out that the emperor was wearing nothing at all, while all his ministers and associates didn't dare say that he was naked as he walked in the procession. Ultimately, it was not just the emperor but everyone associated with him who became a laughing stock before the public.

Scholars have found in a study[42] that as power increases, the tendency to take advice decreases even when it could help the person perform better or make better decisions. This phenomenon of egocentric discounting of advice is also highlighted by Yaniv,[43] though that was in the context of professional advisors.

In many organizations, there are bosses who impose their views and decisions without realizing that these might not be correct or relevant. Often, no one within the organization takes the lead in telling them that they are wrong; instead, people vie with each other to praise those decisions.

Where should the responsibility lie? With the boss who believes that he is the only knowledgeable person in the organization? Or with his subordinates who never point it out to him even when they know he is wrong? It is often possible that the boss is not even aware of his mistakes. If that is the case, the subordinates should try and make him aware of the situation. If they feel that their boss won't listen to them even if they try to convince him, what about the boss's colleagues or his advisers or boss? Will he listen to them? Reporting to the boss's boss may be a good idea but is not always easy because of difficulty in access; further, any direct complaint can be construed as indiscipline or back-biting and create unpleasantness. The best approach then is to tell the boss directly!

Who will bell the boss, if everyone wants to be in his good books?

The dilemma of a group of mice to get rid of a cunning cat is narrated in one of Aesop's fables. They want to tie a bell around the cat's neck so that the cat would not be able to sneak up on and attack them. However, none of the mice volunteered. They kept asking each other, 'Who will bell the cat?'. A similar situation prevails in many organizations, where no one wants to point out the errors of their bosses. Instead of communicating the mistakes of the boss, people like to play safe either by supporting the position taken by the boss or by being a silent spectator of the negative fallouts of his wrong assumptions.

Broadly, there are three factors that can create such a situation:

Systemic level	Personal level	Organizational level
A rigid performance appraisal system that is perceived as boss-centric, crucial, threatening and without easy remedy	**Boss** An individual who is egoistic, unapproachable, stubborn, touchy or illogical	Rigid hierarchical set up that compartmentalizes powers and functions at each level
A top-down work flow system that leaves no room for feedback from below	**Team Member** An individual who is submissive, inert, individualistic, timid, shy or a shameless flatterer	An organizational culture that considers genuine feedback as insubordination or misconduct

A quote attributed to Sydney J. Harris, a columnist of *Chicago Daily News*, is as follows:

'The commonest way to cheat an employer is not by stealing his money or loafing on the job, but by refusing to disagree when you feel he is wrong. If he is paying you for your brains, and not just for your body, an employee has an obligation to dissent from decisions he thinks wrong.'

Prescription for you, the boss

Remember! Your team is your mirror. Allow the team members to express freely what they feel. Otherwise you will not know when others will catch you naked!

Precaution for you

Your commitment should be first to your organization and not to the boss. It is better to be a scapegoat by pointing out the mistake of the boss rather than being a coward or a shameless flatterer.

Precept for the organization

Organizations should evolve and put into practice systems that encourage frank expression of views and opinions.

Appraisal systems should not be overly boss-centric. They should ensure that intolerant bosses do not negatively respond to those who are forthright in their opinions and communicate errors of the bosses.

The signs of recovery

In an environment of accessibility and receptivity, the top management gets the right inputs at the appropriate time for making decisions that are balanced, acceptable and result-oriented.

12

YOU DO THE WORK;
BOSS TAKES THE CREDIT

'MANAGEMENT IS THE art of getting things done' is the oldest and simplest definition of management. Many bosses thrive on this definition and become master delegators. In fact, some may believe

that once elevated to the position of a big boss, one is not expected to work. This is not really true. Even at a very senior level, one has various strategic responsibilities. The acronym POSDCORB, from the management thoughts of Fayol, Gulick and Urwick, talks about the functions of management: Planning, Organizing, Staffing, Directing, Co-ordinating, Reporting and Budgeting. As such, managers at every level have a multitude of tasks related to these functions. There is no justification for the assumption that there is less work at higher levels. If a boss says that he has plenty of spare time, it can mean that he is yet to understand his strategic role.

Why do bosses grab credits that are due to their subordinates?

Mr KSN was elevated to a very senior position in the government, but after he joined the new post, his wife became very unhappy. The reason is that while earlier KSN used to leave well before 8.30 every morning and come back from office around the same time in the evening, after the elevation, he would not leave for office till 11 a.m. and would be back by 5 p.m. In office, he would read newspapers, watch TV, have lunch, take a nap on the sofa, have coffee, and make calls to all his friends and relatives before getting out. His complaint was that he didn't have enough work in his office. That was his wife's complaint too!

What is wrong here? Why would the individual feel that he hasn't got enough work once he was promoted to a new post? Was the organization responsible for this? The primary blame should be on the boss himself. Even after being promoted, he continued with the mind-set of his previous role. He couldn't possibly relate to the new role and what he was expected to do in that position.

In such cases, people noted for their contributions to the organization before being elevated—where they unfortunately perceive less work—like to continue to project their own importance. It is thus very easy to piggyback on the work of their subordinates! Such bosses go to their bosses themselves to present the final output.

There are three categories of bosses who love to take credit for the work of subordinates. First, those who cannot contribute any original work in their position to impress their bosses. The second includes those who have failed in their role and desperately need some achievement to demonstrate to the bosses. The third includes those who believe that their subordinates are performing well only because of them. They claim that but for their substantial contribution, guidance and constant pressure, the team would not have performed the way it did.

There was a CEO in a finance company who had an excellent team of senior executives under him. There were huge arrears in the case of one client which could not be recovered for years. The credit recovery team headed by a young officer came up with a few innovative strategies and legal action, resulting in the recovery of a substantial portion of the outstanding demand. The officer took his team to the CEO, expecting appreciation from him so that his team would also be happy and get motivated. To his surprise, the CEO said, 'Good! But henceforth you should achieve such results without my prompting!' The team went back feeling demotivated and did not have any great achievements to share for several months from that day, but they were re-energized once a new CEO took over!

Awards to the team or to the boss?

An artist, sportsman or a writer can get an award for individual achievements. But can such awards be given to individuals in an organization for their achievements within the organization? They can, if they have made exceptional contributions more than anyone else, and without additional infrastructural support from the organization or its members.

In most organizations, awards and appreciations are given to senior leaders without extending proportionate regards and references to the people behind those leaders' achievements. Most successes happen because of team effort. Of course, there would have been untiring efforts and innovative skills of the leaders behind the success, but that alone would not lead any project to success. Even a small effort by a motivated team member, irrespective of his grade or rank in the organization, should be taken into consideration while gauging the success of his super boss.

A good example is in the Indian Income Tax Department. When an officer in charge of an investigation and assessment passes an order of tax evasion and collects the evaded tax, not only that officer, but everyone below him, right down to staff at the lowest layer in the hierarchy who assisted in the entire process gets rewards proportionate to their contribution and pay. Even the contributions of the bosses who guided him in the work get recognized in the process. However, in many organizations, both in the public and private sectors, rewards, awards and incentives are grabbed by or given to those on top without considering the efforts of the many people below them. This results in frustration, anger and feelings of unfairness among team members. It also damages the future prospects of the organization to achieve better results through team efforts.

Prescription for you, the boss

To be a successful boss, ensure that you appreciate the work of all your team members. Be generous with them and don't remind them of your contribution to the team's success.

Further, take every chance you get to appreciate your team before your bosses. That won't lower your position, but will increase your value as an effective leader. Additionally, your own bosses might learn to do the same thing with you before their bosses.

Precaution for you

Your humility should not prevent you from reporting and projecting your exceptional contribution to the bosses. However, always give credits to your bosses as well. Do not claim appreciation for what you have not done or what you have done as part of your routine job if there is nothing exceptional about it.

Precept for the organization

Do not attribute the credits for success exclusively to the top bosses. Identify contributors at all levels and appreciate them appropriately.

A small pat on the back for specific contributions can sometimes be much more motivating than a routine increase in a pay cheque for many team members. Remember, these are the days when people 'live not by bread' alone.

The signs of recovery

The credibility and popularity of an organization would increase among its employees as and when it starts giving due credits to inputs received from anyone at all levels in the hierarchy.

13

UNETHICAL BOSSES

CLEMENT SAID, 'I joined the corporate sector after working for about 15 years in the armed forces. I was appalled when I observed that my boss wanted his laptop, provided for use in the company, to be removed from the asset register so that he could claim it as his personal item. I objected to it, but he branded me as a wrong man instead.'

An employee who worked with a large international firm returned to his home country because of certain family commitments, and joined a domestic company as a general manager (marketing). However, he quit the job within three months because he could not stomach the unethical practices of the company. He narrated a minor issue among many major ones he refused to divulge: 'The boss used to fake travel bills. I hated this practice as he was not being fair to the company. To make matters worse, he used to encourage others also to prepare and submit fake bills to siphon off money from the company.'

Here is another incident narrated by a junior-level employee of a revenue department: 'When I was posted as an inspector in the Salary Tax Division, I was handed over a file related to fraudulent tax refunds. On perusal I found that the file was incomplete; it did not contain the mandatory order-sheet and related noting. I was asked to file a complaint with the Central Bureau of Investigation without any material to analyse and adduce. Later, my boss called me and reprimanded me in front of my subordinate officers, stating that I had made the case weak. He made me a scapegoat for reasons best known to him.'

Being ethical not only means acting ethically oneself, but also means preventing others from being unethical. It is said that managers who aspire to be ethical must challenge the assumption that they're always unbiased and acknowledge that vigilance, even more than good intention, is a defining characteristic of an ethical manager.[44] An officer from a tax investigation department shared this: 'I was an assistant director and executed a search warrant in the case of a businessman. After searching his premises, I found that all the gold jewellery was accounted for in his tax returns and therefore, nothing needed to be seized. But when I reported this matter to my boss, he told me to seize 10 kg of gold because he needed to achieve his target. I told him it was illegal and unethical to do so, but he didn't listen and orally instructed me to seize the valuables. I was forced to act unethically because of my boss.' There are many such instances in enforcement organizations where bosses ask the subordinate officers to pass orders in whatever ways they want.

One cannot possibly list all types of unethical practices by managers in organizations. But a few widely reported practices are given below:

a) Reporting incorrect facts and figures.
b) Unfair appraisals and favours to people on the basis of gender, religion, caste, region, language or any other consideration.
c) Making incorrect claims for monetary or non-monetary advantages from the organization or others.
d) Taking unethical shortcuts to achieve targets.
e) Making decisions that would benefit them personally.
f) Appropriating resources to oneself unethically.
g) Bribing others to get things done.
h) Sharing or stealing data or invading people's privacy or reputation by snooping and other means.

In an interview, a young chartered accountant said, 'I was the chief accountant in a partnership firm owned by partners who were related to each other. They wanted me to forge documents, hide information about income from the tax department and cheat the clients. After a while I chose to quit.' The manager of an HR company talked about how taking an ethical position could make oneself unwanted with some bosses. He said, 'Once I had to refuse to do some personal work my boss requested due to ethical reasons. He stopped talking to me from that day till I left the organization. That hurt me a lot.'

In a study conducted by the Chartered Management Institute of the UK,[45] it was found that more than one million UK managers felt that they work in an unethical professional environment—30 per cent of them admitted that they are regularly 'ditching ethics' in the organizations they work in. In the 2013 Fraud Survey by EY[46] in Europe, the Middle East, India and Africa, it was reported that 42 per cent of board directors and senior managers were aware of some type of irregular financial reporting in their company, while 57 per cent of respondents felt that corrupt practices were widespread in their companies. Further, the Economic Intelligence Unit and Kroll, a US risk consultancy, have found that 69 per cent of India's companies were affected by fraud in the year 2013.[47] It is significant to note that 89 per cent of the respondents reported that the perpetrator was an insider.

Drouillard and Kleiner stressed the need for a viable moral stance as a necessary prerequisite for a good leader.[48] As one goes up the hierarchy in an organization, there is more freedom to make decisions and more resources at one's disposal. This could make many vulnerable to greed. America's former central banker Alan Greenspan once said, 'It is not that humans have become any more greedy than in generations past. It is that the avenues to express greed have grown enormously.'[49]

An organization with more ethically conscious people can boost its image and can also bring in overall efficiency. On the basis of data collected from 26 CEOs, 71 senior vice-presidents and 185 other organizational members, Berson et al.[50] found that a benevolent CEO resulted in supportive cultures and, in turn, influenced organizational efficiency.

At a juncture where corruption and other unethical practices are ingrained in almost every country and culture, one can expect the same to happen across organizations and more specifically, with the leaders who are at their helm. Transparency International, after collecting data from 114000 respondents in 107 countries, reported in 2013[51] that 27 per cent of the respondents stated that they had paid a bribe in the last 12 months. Further, during a survey conducted by the consulting firm Deloitte Forensic (India) in 2014,[52] a majority of respondents stated that 'they would not feel comfortable working for a company that is perceived as indulging in corrupt practices'.

Though there could be debate over what is ethical and what is not, one has to go by the normative framework of the society that is ubiquitous at the time. An ethical position has an overwhelming influence over all other things, however scientific, sophisticated and popular they are. Undoubtedly, a person who always strives to conform to ethical values can become a role model in any organization.

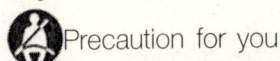Prescription for you, the boss

If you indulge in any unethical practices, you can expect many others down the line to follow your footsteps more aggressively. You leave a trail of whatever you do in the organization. When you are in the seat, no one would act against you. But as soon as you are out, there might be many who rush to expose the 'skeletons in your cupboard'.

Precaution for you

How not to be a party to the unethical practices of the boss? You can try to keep away from assisting the boss in unethical acts and by refusing to take any benefit out of such practices.

Further, do not act on oral directions of unethical bosses. Document all instructions and be bold enough to be a whistle-blower if the unethical activities of the boss can greatly harm the organization.

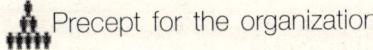Precept for the organization

Company management should demonstrate to everyone in the organization that it is serious about curbing unethical practices.

This can happen only when the organization itself is a torchbearer of ethical practices in its domain. The organization should take direct, immediate, and exemplary action to punish offenders. Its vigilance and ethical compliance units should engage in continuous monitoring of activities, especially of those in sensitive and vulnerable positions, and suggest appropriate action to the top management. Finally, organizations should follow corporate governance regulations and the norms for business ethics scrupulously and reward ethical managers.

The signs of recovery

Ethical leaders have enduring popularity and can nurture an ethically conscious team. Organizations with such people can become role models for good business and governance.

> **10 commandments for people who work under an unethical boss**
> 1. Keep a healthy distance
> 2. Avoid getting introduced to his personal friends
> 3. Get his instructions and orders in writing
> 4. Don't give access to your personal communication devices or platforms such as mobile phones, tablets or email accounts to the boss to communicate with outsiders.
> 5. Avoid going for non-official parties hosted by him
> 6. Don't take any personal obligations from him
> 7. Be careful not to be a party in his unethical dealings
> 8. Report to appropriate seniors if you find things getting out of control in terms of unethical acts
> 9. Warn others against falling prey to the boss's unethical practices
> 10. Get out of that position at the earliest opportunity

> **Popular perceptions of honest bosses**
>
> Fundamental belief: Honesty is the most likeable quality.
> Popular perception: Honest bosses are not always likeable. Honest

bosses are fundamentalist, unsophisticated, unpleasant and rude. They are rule-bound, bookish and overly matter-of-fact in response. They don't condone mistakes or allow for deviations. Even when they are polite, they tend to be passive-aggressive instead of really helping the erring ones.

Fundamental belief: Honesty is the best policy.
Popular perception: Having an honest boss can be a real irritant. He can be arrogant when he makes it clear that certain things are just not possible.

Fundamental belief: Honesty is a virtue.
Popular perception: Honest bosses are boring. Some even fuss when they are invited to a party or given a drink. Even if they agree, they are likely to put conditions about other invitees. They are tight-lipped. They behave as if others would steal their ideas. They listen to all conversations and choose not to contribute anything to discussions.

Fundamental belief: Honesty comes out of wisdom.
Popular perception: Honest persons are fools. They are impractical and fail to make use of opportunities. There is no point putting them in powerful positions.

Fundamental belief: Honesty comes out of a brave heart.
Popular perception: Honest people are scared to act.

Fundamental belief: Honesty should be rewarded.
Popular perception: Honest bosses should be made answerable for even a small error of judgement. They should be thrown out at the first chance; indeed, many would love to see them fall.

Fundamental belief: Honesty is to be taught.
Popular perception: No one wants to listen to the sermons of an

honest boss. It is no fun interacting with him.

Fundamental belief: Honesty is respected.
Popular perception: What is there to respect in an honest boss? He refuses to budge when he is requested to.

Fundamental belief: Honesty is a rare quality.
Popular perception: It is disgusting to see the honest boss who tries to swim against the wave. If the entire system is dishonest, what is the use of an honest boss raising a red flag?

Fundamental belief: Honesty leads to enduring success.
Popular perception: The projects and initiatives of honest bosses should be shot down as they don't work in today's world.

Fundamental belief: Honesty gives one a good reputation.
Popular perception: Honest bosses do honest things for gaining good reputations only. So they should also be defamed.

Fundamental belief: Like William Shakespeare said: 'No legacy is as rich as honesty'.
Popular perception: Honest bosses will indeed die poor; they may smile in their graves and beyond, but what purpose does it serve?

Conclusion
People love honesty; but don't know how to deal with honest people. Still it is worth it to be honest!

14

THE COTERIE RULES; NOT THE BOSS

BOSSES OFTEN CAN and do seek the help of trusted loyalists. However, what if the boss is dependent on them for every small decision? Or what if the members take advantage and start trying to control everything the boss does?

There are three types of bosses that encourage and nurture coteries. The first includes those who are not comfortable with members in the existing team. Though they are placed in a position where they have people with specialized roles to assist them, they would like to work only with people they are comfortable with. They might redefine existing roles and give key portfolios to their favourites. If a change of portfolios is not possible, they might ignore and bypass existing incumbents and seek to work only with their favourites. The second type consists of those who completely depend on their team members. They are unable to take independent decisions, thus the team members decide everything and the bosses simply put their stamp at the final stage. The third type of bosses are those who nurture a group of individuals from outside the team. They could be people who worked with him earlier or a group of trusted friends. These members follow the bosses wherever they go!

Why do some bosses want 'Man Fridays'?

Coteries wield extensive powers in some organizations. The bosses spend substantial time discussing and gossiping with their trustworthy associates and they enjoy the courtesies not given even to those higher than them in the hierarchy. Though everyone hates a coterie that controls their bosses, many seek their assistance in getting things done.

A boss under the clutches of a coterie is usually not popular in the organization. The legitimacy of his authority and decisions, if any, is often challenged. Even if he takes a fair decision, he can be accused of being partisan and parochial.

Mrs Lakshmi was heading a large organization. She was always surrounded by a few lady colleagues who gave her information on all the happenings within the organization. They would spend hours discussing and analysing personal matters of other members and arrive at their own judgements. Gradually, the coterie began influencing Mrs Lakshmi in all her decisions, which created a lot of heartburn within the organization as other colleagues started getting side-lined. Needless to say, the boss lost her popularity and had to face an investigation on complaints of unfairness.

According to the leader–member exchange theory, there is a dyadic relationship between leaders and followers. Earlier, it was assumed that leaders behaved, treated and responded to all employees similarly. However, it has been found that this does not happen in reality. Within an organization, the leader can perceive an in-group and out-group, with the members of the in-group being his loyalists. They are the ones who receive gains from the leader directly or indirectly, or who expect some sort of benefit in the future.

Bob Frisch, an author and a consultant for several Fortune 500 companies for several decades, says that though there are formal decision-making bodies in many of these organizations, decisions are indeed often taken by someone else. He lists some of the virtues of the 'kitchen cabinet'[53] as a) it frees the CEO from the tyranny of the organizational chart, b) small groups are much better than large ones for taking critical decisions and c) people can't easily lobby since they are unaware of the exact identity of the group.

A few trustworthy friends or associates are necessary for every individual. However, that cannot come to mean that all decisions are influenced by these persons. One should not be dependent on a coterie; a leader doing so would not get acceptability in the team and his decisions would not be considered fair.

There is a saying 'Show me your friend, I will show you what you will become'. Some friends can be instrumental in one's growth and some can be responsible for one's decline. There have been leaders who were forced to resign from their posts because they were associated with or accused of being influenced by tainted persons. The coterie, especially if it is from outside the organization, can be seen as more dangerous.

> **Questions to you, the boss**
>
> Are you influenced by a coterie?
> If yes, what type of a boss are you?
> - One who allows your favourite loyalists to influence you
> - One who feels helpless without the support of a coterie and follows their advice most of the time
> - One who is influenced by a group of individuals outside the existing team
>
> If your answer is YES to any of the above questions, you are indeed in a weak position, and need to re-look at your ways of working.

> **Questions for you to ponder**
>
> - Do you think your boss encourages a coterie because you keep your distance from him?
> - Do you think your boss takes support of a coterie, because he is a weak leader?
> - Do you think the ultimate gain is for the members of the coterie and not for the boss?

15

THE CHATTERBOX

THERE ARE PEOPLE who are fond of talking all the time, on any topic under the sun. They tend to make the atmosphere light and energetic, but may end their work day without much value creation. We have already discussed the saying that as a person goes up the organizational hierarchy, he has more time and less work. However, this is not applicable only to the seniors; many bosses at middle and other levels also find chatting a good pastime in their offices.

This is an asset as well as a liability. While they can make friends easily, a lot of valuable time is wasted through unnecessary sharing of views and opinions about anyone and anything. When I was in

college, I used to paste a small slip on my hostel room door that said, 'I like chatting; but not now!'. It was my strategy to avoid some of my chatterbox friends when I was busy; it was not to escape chatting altogether, but to prioritize and allocate appropriate time for every task.

According to the blabbermouth theory of leadership, those who talk the loudest or the longest would become the leader. This is not really true. People expect and appreciate quality in conversations of a leader, rather than quantity. A person becomes ineffective if he indulges in what some people call 'verbal diarrhoea'. The tongue deserves rest so that the mind and ears can be directed towards internalizing the ideas and actions of others.

Some bosses do not hesitate to extend their chat to extreme personal levels. Avila, an HR trainer, had this to share: 'My boss had no sense of boundaries at work. He would freely mingle and get personal with the trainees. This was a bone of contention in our team. One day, he attended one of my sessions where we were playing a learning game, took over and twisted the game into the personal arena. Trainees and I were made to ask intimate personal questions. Oh, what a showdown we had in the team room later that day!'

Time spent on the phone

Some bosses are known for engaging in long conversations over the phone in spite of the fact that there are many important and impatient visitors waiting. Even if the listener might enjoy the chats of the boss, he has to put up with too much talk sometimes.

Recently, I had to visit a government office for urgent work. Thanks to the outsourcing wave, the reception was manned by a private security guard. He was on the free telephone, chatting with someone very intimately. I tried clearing my throat loudly to catch his attention, which is when he looked up, reluctantly cut the call, and gestured to me. He gave me the room number of the officer I had to meet.

Since there was no guard in the vicinity, I gently opened the door to the officer's room. The officer was on the phone; I smiled at him while he just looked through me. I took a few steps inside. We had not met before, which could have been the reason for his continued attention to the talker at the other end of his telephone. I expected him to gesture to me to sit. However, on realizing that he was very amused by the incoming gossip and also in a mood to part with his own contributions, I left the room. I walked slowly, expecting a call asking me to stay back. It did not happen, so I went out. Most of the staff were busy talking, either on landlines or cellphones.

After a while, I went to the officer and found that *sahib* was still on a call. As his concentration and involvement with me during these conversations were at their worst, I closed the door and came out again. It had been about an hour since I had entered this office for the first time. I went in search of one my colleagues who also worked in that office. Fortunately, she was available and very happily welcomed me with surprise—we were meeting after many years. As I sat, she ordered coffee and enquired where I was posted and the purpose of my visit. Just as I opened my mouth to answer, one of her telephones rang. She answered and said 'Yes Ma'am', 'Right Ma'am', 'Okay Ma'am', continuously for about 15 minutes. Meanwhile, other phones in the room were also ringing at alternate intervals. As she was about to sip the coffee, which was cold by then, and as I was about to answer her first query, her phone rang again. The voice from the other side was so loud that I could hear the lady. My colleague told me that it was her batchmate calling from the other side of the country and continued the conversation. They were discussing various topics that seemingly amused both of them, such as promotion prospects, recent divorces and separations among colleagues, problems with domestic servants and mothers-in-law, womanizing bosses, nutty lady bosses and kids' homework. Even after about 25 minutes of chatting (all the while smiling and winking at me as if I was also a subject of discussion or an active participant in the conversation), she was not in a mood to end the call. At one point, her cellphone rang and she quickly glanced at the number and said, 'Call from kids. They want my help for homework.' Providentially, my mobile rang so I excused myself and escaped from the room. I peeped in once again to see whether the officer was free, but found him still chatting over the phone.

It is good news that telecommunications has become the lifeline for individuals and organizations today because they are cheap and omnipresent. But it is bad news that it is not used by people at the correct place and time, or for the relevant task and for the required duration.

In a study conducted by Vodafone UK,[54] it was found that 65 per cent of managers do not mind staff doing personal things like calling family members or checking social networking sites as long as they get all their work done. At the same time, most of these managers—may be as a 'quid pro quo'—wanted their employees to extend their working hours.

Bosses should be role models in demonstrating to the team the value of time as well as the need to be judicious while engaging in telephonic conversations at the workplace, whether they are made for official or personal purposes.

Prescription for you, the boss

It is written in proverbs that 'A truly wise person uses few words; a person with understanding is even-tempered'. Bosses need to demonstrate competency and warmth not through many words but through 'short and sweet' interactions. If you don't value your time in the organization, no one else will.

Precaution for you

Don't encourage a chatterbox boss by contributing to spice up his unending chats. At the earliest opportunity, drive home the point that you need him to address your issues. Avoid frequent, unneccessary interactions with chronic 'chatters'.

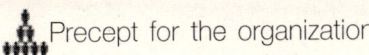

Precept for the organization

Establish an organizational culture that discourages long personal calls at the workplace.

Create a convention of conducting meetings with proper agendas and without unnecessary digressions, but in a friendly and pleasant environment.

The signs of recovery

Effective leaders believe in the famous quote, 'An ounce of doing is better than a ton of talking'. Also, that does not deter them from listening to the people who approach them with problems.

16

THE PLEASE-ALL BOSS

WE HAVE TALKED about bosses who are unapproachable; however, there are some bosses who are just the opposite. They are extremely receptive to all and sundry and have difficulty discouraging anybody who walks into their chambers. They wish to be popular and can never 'call a spade a spade'. There is an eagerness to gather information and gossip, and they cannot help wasting time listening to unproductive conversations. They are also indecisive because of their 'please-all' trait. They may eulogize the actions of their colleagues even when they clearly know that there have been mistakes made. They are usually ineffective leaders as they are also scared to correct their subordinates.

Many please-all bosses can also be hypocritical in behaviour, and tend to hide their actual perceptions or views from others. An employee of a leading manufacturing firm was very happy with his boss who used to praise his work. But one day, he came to know that his boss used to share his (the employee's) shortcomings with another person in the hierarchy. When that person told the employee about this, he felt dejected and wondered why his boss didn't point out his mistakes to him directly.

A leader needs to be acceptable, but he is not out to win a popularity contest. He need not be on a frantic mission to please everyone around him all the time. He has to be straightforward and frank in his verbal and non-verbal communication. Quoting Hart and Quinn, Sean T. Hannab et al. argued, 'To be effective, leaders may require kindness or forgiveness in one situational role and persistence and vitality in another—perhaps within the span of minutes, requiring behavioural flexibility.'[55]

Yearning for approval stems from lack of self-confidence

John succeeded Jay as the senior vice-president of a large biotech company. While Jay had been known for his no-nonsense approach towards the employees, John became an instant hit for his cordial behaviour with everyone. Jay never tolerated indiscipline or lethargy at work; John never reprimanded anyone and even supported them if they came up with an excuse for not completing a particular project on time. Over time, John's seniors found his approach corroding the productivity of the company. Most of the hard-working managers who worked with him found his approach silly and petty. It was also found that he had ridiculed the stiff targets set by the management in front of members, in his effort to please the employees' union. He was relieved of his duties immediately.

It is observed that many people who like to please others are the ones who lack confidence in themselves. They seek public approval for their acts and are reluctant to disagree with the views of others. They tend to get worried about what others think about them; due to this, they are quite lenient and rarely disapprove of others' actions. A boss who is always in a 'please-all' state of mind can thus end up promising things that may not be easy to deliver, due to many organizational constraints, procedural issues or precedents. This in turn results in undue stress on the members and the boss losing credibility among the employees. Linda D. Tillman[56], a clinical psychologist, has stated that for many people the word 'No' drops out of their vocabulary; they substitute it with ways to make other people happy. According to her, there are three types of 'No': The unassertive 'No' (weak excuses and lacking confidence); the aggressive 'No' (may include an attack on the person making the request), and the assertive 'No' (which is simple and direct).

When team members find that they have a please-all boss, it is likely that some of them exploit or manipulate him. A please-all boss can easily fall prey to their designs, resulting in unfair decisions, in turn making him unpopular in the organization. Further, he can get into trouble for violating established practices. Harriet B. Braiker, a clinical psychologist and management consultant, has said that people-pleasing is a 'disease'[57] and one has to cure oneself of it by bringing in appropriate changes in thoughts, feelings and behaviour.

℞ Prescription for you, the boss

You can be cordial, gentle, and receptive to the team, but that does not mean you should be on a popularity mission and try to please each and every member all the time. Making people happy is a good quality. But the attempt to please everyone would be counter-productive and your credibility will go for a toss. You can even be accused of not being credible, fair or confident. Be assertive in your response to the actions, suggestions, and requests of others. Be wise enough to know when to say 'yes' and when to say 'no'.

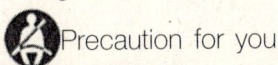

Precaution for you

Don't get carried away by the responses of a please-all boss. He cannot be fair and genuine in his judgements. You need to introspect about your competence, output and views. Try to get more objective views and advice from others—such as colleagues or mentors—before getting thrilled by the response of a please-all boss.

Precept for the organization

Identify the please-all bosses in the organization. While they might have a happy and contented set of followers, there could also be indiscipline, inefficiency and cynicism against the organizational goals, along with reduced productivity. There is also a possibility that these bosses generate negative feelings among team members about the taskmasters in the organization. There should be a check on the activities and approaches of all bosses to ensure fairness, discipline and efficiency in the organization.

The signs of recovery

When the please-all leadership style is replaced by a firm and fair approach, the sincere and committed ones in the team get motivated to put in their best and the shirkers and flatterers lose ground.

17

WHERE THERE IS A WILL, THERE IS A LOAD!

MOST PEOPLE WILL agree that the more willing you are to work, the more load you will be dumped with. This is a common grievance of many sincere workers in the organization. Bosses prefer such 'donkeys' who won't grumble when more work is given to them.

Being the boss's favourite because you work a lot does not mean you will get any special privileges when compared to those who shirk work. Hard-working people who do not object to an additional workload are often denied leave even in an emergency. Bosses may start thinking of them as indispensable and feel insecure when the toilers are away from work even for a few hours.

Shyam, a very enterprising and systematic person, was a middle-level manager who always exceeded targets. His boss depended on him to realize the overall target. Shyam was a workaholic and at the beck and call of his boss, even on holidays and after office hours. One Friday afternoon, he had to leave office early to make arrangements for a ceremony connected with the birth of his son. He took permission to go home at 2 p.m. But when he came back on Monday, the administrative officer handed him a note from the boss on the file. He had written, 'Since the officer had left before 2 p.m., ask him to apply for leave for half a day.' Shyam was in a state of shock. He had plenty of leaves left; that was not an issue. What upset him was the attitude of his boss. He recalled how many extra hours he had worked in that office, and how many weekends he had come to help the boss to clear the pending workload of the entire office! Why should his boss be petty and write such a remark on the file?

The above incident is a classic example of how intelligent donkeys are exploited by their bosses. Over time, this trend has been a lesson to those who are sincere and hard-working but shrewd, teaching them not to demonstrate their eagerness before exploitative bosses. When asked to do a job, they may plead ignorance even when they are experts in that topic. The only way they can express their unwillingness is by doing so. Ultimately it is a loss for the organization.

The free riders and loafers

As seen above, in an exploitative environment led by inefficient bosses, it is the intelligent people who fail to contribute their best for fear of excessive extraction of their time and energy. If the boss is efficient, he can ensure that tasks are distributed among team members in an equitable manner, such that everyone in the team is properly equipped to contribute his best in an optimal way. This is not to deny the fact that there would be people of differing capability and potential in an organization. Both practices, namely, putting the entire load on willing team members or allowing unwilling team members to continue in their lazy ways are the hallmarks of inefficient and easygoing bosses.

Organizations in the government and public sector are notorious for a pattern that results in continuous loading of work on sincere employees. This is because there is nothing they can do about the free riders, loafers and inefficient lot that constitute a majority of the workforce. These organizations can neither reduce their pay nor send them out due to archaic, impractical and unfair job contracts. Ultimately, the sufferers are those who are committed to updating their skills and contributing their best. For some, it is not only commitment, but also values of respect, loyalty and obedience that are ingrained in their personality that make them work. They continue working irrespective of their bosses. In fact, like the 80–20 rule (law of the vital few) of Pareto,[58] many government organizations engaged in public service still stay afloat, even if not as efficiently as some of the private sector organizations, only because of a handful of sincere souls at various levels.

Though equitable work allocation is unrealistic in any organization due to disparities in expertise, potential and aptitude, there needs to be proper distribution of workload at each level. Even in new-generation organizations where there is scientific screening and allocation of work at the entry level, the process can get diluted at subsequent levels. In a competitive and fast business environment, organizations often need to depend on those who deliver quickly and efficiently; at the same time, they must also take care to compensate members for extra efforts. Further, in terms of overall and enduring productivity of the organization, it should be understood that monetary incentives alone cannot provide motivation. Ultimately, faced with health hazards, family expectations and relationship strains, hard-working executives would not enjoy even the most exciting tasks or opportunities.

What is the solution? Don't kill the goose that lays the golden egg!

Bosses need to understand that there are wise people around them. If the bosses throw their loads in frustration, there may not be anyone to pick up the same. They must, therefore, ensure that they utilize the sincere members but don't squeeze them. A true leader is the one who creates meaningful tasks in an environment such that people hasten to shoulder the responsibilities assigned to them.

Equitable allocation of the workload, distribution of meaningful tasks according to the aptitude and potential of the employees and setting realistic targets at every level would result in overall organizational well-being. Employees need to understand that pleading ignorance before an exploitative boss is not a solution. That would make them not only unwanted but also underutilized, which would ultimately harm their creativity and performance. They need to be receptive to the extent the organization needs them and also to the extent they can demonstrate their potential.

Prescription for you, the boss

Don't overload the hard-workers and write off the loafers and free riders. The more the latter are in number, the more inefficient you will be perceived. A true leader is the one who creates tasks for everyone according to their capabilities and aptitudes.

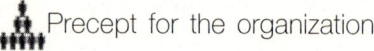Precaution for you

Pleading ignorance to an exploitative boss is not a true remedy and can affect your creativity. Remember, opportunities are gateways to great accomplishments.

Precept for the organization

Organizations need to self-introspect: Is the workload equitably distributed? Are tasks assigned logically? Are the targets realistic?

Putting excessive strain on willing team members will only boomerang on the organizations and will not help the members either. Don't take hard-workers for granted.

The signs of recovery

Positive perceptions about equity along with recognition can lead to better organizational commitment and an environment of exemplary work ethics.

18

WHY DOESN'T THE BOSS SMILE?

IN MANY ORGANIZATIONS, one can easily spot a boss who tends to think of his smile as a treasure that cannot be showered on all and sundry. He may believe that his serious expression, along with measured words, gives him an edge over others and shows his

superiority. He prefers to get straight to business and targets during one-to-one meetings, and doesn't exude warmth to the employee or visitor. There are others who may get out of the car and walk straight into their cabins without even responding to the respectful and friendly wishes of their employees.

Bosses do not become so overnight; it is a process where people are given the top job over a period of time by virtue of merit or seniority in the organization. Employees and other stakeholders, therefore, naturally expect better understanding and empathy from a boss coming up from within the organization. Of course, a certain degree of change in the interaction pattern is tolerable even if not always desirable. For example, the boss may leave the luncheon circles where he used to be an active member. He may stop cracking jokes with his erstwhile colleagues and may not seem to enjoy their conversations any more. Leaders who move up fast in the hierarchy should not forget that their behavioural pattern in the pre-boss phase is known to many in the organization.

Bosses need to shed their aura

Organizations have managers vertically positioned and the pyramidal structure is inevitable for both coordination and discipline. As a person moves up in the hierarchy, he tends to make incremental additions to his aura at every stage, often becoming inaccessible and formal. Bosses need to realize that the backbone of the organization is its employees. All calculations regarding performance, targets and success depend on the quality of work put in by them. Even if the organization provides all performance-linked incentives and a number of amenities, one good gesture from the boss will definitely motivate the subordinates more than anything else.

Gianpiero Petriglieri and Mark Stein,[59] in their article in *Organization Studies* describe what they call 'The Unwanted Self' to refer to the projective identification in a leader's identity work. According to them, 'while the leaders are likely to work hard to actualise and maintain selves that reflect' what is valued by team members, there also 'exists a reservoir of selves that they do not like or wish to become'. Looking from this perspective, the demonstration of 'seriousness' and 'arrogance' may be a perverse way of gaining and exerting power.

Dealing with the public

Even in organizations engaged in public services like telecom, power, insurance and welfare where people largely throng with grievances, bosses and the designated public relations officers need to be more responsive. Public opinion will be more positive if the officer gives people a warm welcome and patient hearing even when the grievance is not fully resolved. Sadly, currently the public is too scared to even make a telephone call to such organizations, due to the largely rude and impatient responses.

Smile goes a mile

Machiavelli's dictum for leaders is: Be feared than be loved. That would not be applicable in modern organizational settings. Warmth and kindness will make bosses more popular and respected in the organization. Those who believe in demonstrating 'busy boss' behaviour and a 'bosses mean only business' attitude are definitely mistaken. Gone are the days when one could extract work from subordinates through fear or an undue manifestation of authority. Present-day employees expect understanding, empathy and encouragement.

℞ Prescription for you, the boss

You are mistaken if you believe that people will respect you for the seriousness on your face. That is not an indicator of the power and responsibility you claim to shoulder. Your team members and the public do not care whether you are toiling with a great problem or brainstorming on a path-breaking business plan to save the company. They expect a pleasant expression and response from you when they meet you or interact with you.

Precaution for you

Do not get upset if your boss never smiles at anybody, including you. For some, it is in their nature not to smile; that does not prevent you from smiling at them, especially if the person is your boss. In fact, it is possible that you could make your boss smile with your smile!

 Precept for the organization

Organizations should ensure that they have people with pleasing personalities in cutting-edge positions both at the top, where they need to address large teams or large gatherings, as well as in the front end, where they need to meet the public face-to-face. Both of these kinds of people represent not only themselves but also the organization as responsive, communicative, and approachable.

The signs of recovery

Pleasant bosses make for happy employees; consequently, the organization will also transmit a culture of openness and receptivity.

19

PREDECESSOR BASHING: WHAT FOOLISH BOSSES DO!

THERE IS A joke in a large organization in the context of leadership transitions. A new CEO, after taking over, asked the parting CEO for advice regarding potential issues. The latter said: 'Whenever there is a problem, open the desk drawer where there are three envelopes containing advice; those will guide you.' When faced with the first problem after taking over, the new CEO opened the first envelope. It was written 'Blame the predecessor'. After a few months he faced another serious issue. He opened the next envelope to get advice. 'Restructure', it mentioned in bold letters. A year later, when facing another problem, the CEO opened the third envelope to read: 'Prepare three envelopes'.

It is often commonly noticed that the new incumbent blames the predecessor for every disorder or problem at work. Further, this is done in a very refined manner. Even though he showers praise on the predecessor in public meetings or compliments his unique initiatives when the team members are around, in private he loves criticizing the predecessor.

It is likely that certain business and professional commitments were made to various stakeholders by the predecessor. Contracts were signed, decisions were taken and cooperation was extended based on certain written or unwritten promises, which were within the parameters of laws and convention. Though such strategies were used in the best interest of the organization, predecessor bashers may mercilessly break all such promises. This results in loss of trust and a consequent dent in organizational credibility with the stakeholders. Stiff targets might have also been fixed by the predecessor, with the promise that appropriate support systems would be provided to each division. However, the successor boss may fail to take into consideration such promises and assess the results while claiming that he is impartial. This can create dissatisfaction and disappointment in the team.

If each successive boss changes the strategies of the organization according to his whims and fancies, there will not be any consistency, stability or clarity. If the successor makes a 'U-turn' in approach and strategy, the result would be chaos and confusion.

Monarchs, generals, ambassadors, and governors

By making transitions smooth, organizations can reduce any possible strain if the successor wants to bring in an entirely new policy. Many top bosses, by virtue of their long and responsible tenure with the organization, nurture an emotional chord for a long time. In the book *Hero's Farewell*, Jeffrey Sonnenfeld has examined the role of a CEO's departure style on helping or hindering the transfer of power.[60] He identified four major types of leadership departure styles: Monarchs, who choose not to leave voluntarily but either die in office or are overthrown; Generals, who leave reluctantly and spend their retirement planning a comeback; Ambassadors, who retain close ties with their former organizations; and Governors, who willingly serve a limited time and leave to pursue new interests.

A few desirable steps during a leadership transition

Apart from the mandatory and formal hand-over documents, every organization should establish practices where informal interactions take place between the predecessor and successor and the core team. This is so as to create a link between the predecessor's and successor's views, policies and strategies as well as to understand the environment, background and existing vision.

Some desirable steps are given below:

- Detailed and well-structured departure meetings at both formal and informal levels.
- Detailed briefing on the projects in progress
- Updates about initiatives in the pipeline
- Any threats; identified or suspected
- Introduction of key team members
- Knowledge-transfer on key strategic areas developed by the predecessor
- Discussion of the successor's future plans with the predecessor.

In the case of very top bosses, organizations may also consider keeping them on as mentors or board members for some time.

℞ Prescription for you, the boss

You might have very innovative and successful business and professional strategies for the new organization. You might have also understood the blunders and deficiencies the new organization made earlier. However, that should not mean that you criticize everything done in the past and quickly undo whatever has already been established. Even if your steps are justified, in the best interest of the organization and required to be implemented immediately, you should make efforts to convince the entire team about the desirability of the changes. You should use it as an opportunity to demonstrate leadership skills, by garnering support from the members. You can do this by presenting views and strategies without picking faults in the earlier ones. Such an approach can even elicit a compliment from the predecessor.

Precaution for you

A good leader will always admit to mistakes and setbacks. Most importantly, at the time of leaving the organization, he should be in a retrospective mood rather than simply celebrating achievements. The leader should carefully evaluate past strategies and brief the successor about their strengths and weaknesses. He should also warn the latter on the possible fallouts of past decisions and steps that can be taken to reduce the damage. He can make a SWOT analysis and share this with the successor. Further, he can document the circumstances in which certain decisions or commitments had to be made, so that no one can question his intentions or accuse him of wrongdoing later.

20

COPING WITH A YOUNG BOSS

SAINT-SAENS WAS A child prodigy. At the age of two and a half, he picked up the perfect pitch on his piano and composed his first piece at the age of three. It is said that Hector Berlioz, the famous French romantic composer who lived in the 1800s, did an objective assessment of this brilliant young composer after his first symphony. When asked for a feedback he said, 'He knows everything, but lacks experience.' This is precisely what some old team members say about their young bosses too.

The phenomenon of the generation gap is universal and present since time immemorial. It exists in all types of entities, from the family to large corporates to governments. The difference is that while there were only two broad categories earlier, namely, the old and the young, there are now four categories with distinguishable characteristics and attitudes: old, middle-aged, young, and entry level. Ron Maxie, Claire Raines and Bob Filipczak in their book *Generations at Work* call them Veterans, Boomers, Xers, and Nexters.[61] There are a few other scholars who categorized the generations at work based on the period of their birth: Traditionalists (born before 1945), Baby boomers (born between 1946 and 1964), Generation-X (born between 1965 and 1976) and Generation-Y (born between 1977 and 1994). Now, one more category has been widely recognized—Generation-Z, which refers to those born after 1994.

Many organizations recruit people at senior levels directly. Government organizations also have young people coming to top positions through lateral recruitment. As multiple generations work in the same organization, there are bound to be issues. Apart from the conflicts related to differing perceptions in sociological, professional and technological realms, there are a lot of misunderstandings that can occur around attitudes and behavioural patterns at personal levels. Older employees may accuse the young ones of taking hasty decisions without fully comprehending the intricacies and complexities of the problems. At the same time, the young ones may feel that 'angels have to rush in where fools fear to tread', that is, sometimes haste must be made.

Youngsters may further ask why veterans sit late in the office and yet show little progress in their work. The older ones, sticklers to the rules, may accuse the younger members for not adhering to prescribed office timings, making the latter wonder why the 'oldies' spend so much time in talking and showering unwanted advice.

Older team members often believe that they are more loyal to the organization by virtue of their long tenure. They may feel that the young bosses are like fair-weather friends and lack long-term commitment to the organization.

Young bosses are usually the product of outstanding achievements early in life. Most of them have the following characteristic features that distinguish them from the older team members.

- They have enthusiasm to implement their creative ideas
- They are technocrats and want application of the latest technology at work
- They are cyber-wizards
- They desire radical changes, look for challenges and like to experiment
- Their role models are mostly young, living persons
- They're uncomfortable with conventional timings to work in
- They want quick implementation of projects
- Personal life and pleasures are as important as a career
- They are for creating new rules
- They welcome alternate careers

'How could he shout at me? I am twice as old as him!' GK, a senior manager who spent more than 35 years with a financial institution, wept like a child. He sat in a park alone during the lunch break. The incident that had happened in the morning disturbed him very much. He was called to the chamber by the young boss and shouted at in front of two other colleagues. The boss yelled: 'What nonsense have you done while processing the housing project of the client? Aren't you ashamed of your lack of understanding even after completing the so-called "rich" bl---y years in this organization?' The young boss was not patient enough to listen to GK's explanation. He believed that he was right in his decision and behaviour. This attitude hurt GK deeply. 'I have never cried even once after I have grown up. But this man made me cry today.'

Why did GK's young boss behave in a hurtful manner? Was it proper of him to shout so rudely at an employee much older in age and experience in the organization? Many of GK's colleagues discussed this in private. They were of the view that the boss needed to respect the age of the subordinates and talk to them respectfully. However, often young bosses do not believe in such courtesies. They believe that there is no consideration required for age or experience when enforcing discipline and efficiency at work.

Young bosses are not just whiffs of fresh air, they are there to bring paradigm shifts in the organization. They are able to make use of the latest technology in providing speedy and better strategic solutions. The tectonic shift in working style may wreck the boats of senior employees. However, they cannot take a large experienced workforce for granted while conceiving and implementing new plans and projects.

℞ Prescription for you, the 'young' boss

You may be better educated, technologically brilliant, healthier and more energetic than the experienced team members in your organization. However, that is no excuse for riding roughshod over them. Go out of your way to elicit their opinions, discern their area of strengths and competencies and make them believe that you too belong with them. Don't shy away from exercising control over them but reserve your iron fist for the recalcitrant only.

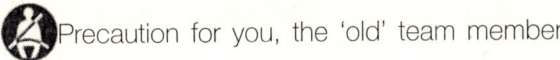Precaution for you, the 'old' team member

Understand that your boss is from a different generation and may have a different upbringing. He may have a different perception of a career and life and might be brimming with creative ideas that could solve some of the challenges the organization faces. Adopt a positive attitude and try to understand his style of working, even if it is very different from yours.

Precept for the organization

The hierarchical structure and reporting mechanism established in the organization should factor in the inherent differences in the nature and expectations of each age group at work. It should create an environment that facilitates open communication and team work between the old and young workforce. Appropriate training may be given to each generational category to reduce prejudices and stereotyped notions.

The signs of recovery

As young leaders build organizations on the bedrock of a mature and stable past, the veterans can approach innovative and radical ideas with a positive attitude.

21

COPING WITH AN OLD BOSS

AT A LEADERSHIP session, while interacting with young graduates from top business schools who joined the management of various companies, it was observed that a majority of them said, 'We are fed up of hearing oft-repeated statements from our bosses.'

Some of these statements are:

- 'In our days, we had to share cubicles with others, yet we had excellent focus in work'
- 'We used to walk miles to reach school'
- 'We came in our old bikes to the office'
- 'We were always earlier than our bosses in the office and went home only after they had left'
- 'We always took a printout and handed over a report personally'
- 'We never used to have chewing gum, while you people blow bubbles in the office'
- 'How could you sit on the sofa and work? We never used to get up from the assigned seat'
- 'How can you focus on work with those wires connected to both ears? We also used to listen to music, but not when we were at office'

Young managers will only have contempt for comments like the ones listed above. They point out that times have changed and so should the methodologies and attitudes. They believe that the principles and postulates upheld and repeated by old bosses are not worthy of emulation; at least some of them.

Younger leaders tend to look askance at the following beliefs of their elders:

- Learning happens through experience
- The more senior you are, the more wise and mature you are
- Rules are products of wisdom of the past—these are sacrosanct and not to be meddled with
- Build the present based on past experiences
- Resources and technology should be used till they last; economic prudence takes precedence over modernization
- Focus on stability and continuity, rapid changes are risky

Young managers may dislike disingenuous anecdotes based on experiences narrated by their bosses. As against the above, youngsters believe that learning can happen through many ways apart from experience. It is not correct to assume that young managers are immature and seniors always behave in a mature manner. One needs to bypass outdated practices and procedures if they no longer serve the cause of the organization. It is necessary to think and act 'out-of-the-box' in the best interest of the organization. That can pave the way for new laws, replacing archaic, irrelevant and ineffective rules and procedures. Further, younger members may feel that in a multitasking environment, the organization requires the best infrastructure and resources. Technology needs to be replaced for better output without waiting for it to become obsolete.

While many belonging to the older generation show admirable adroitness in dealing with the challenges posed by new technologies, there are countless others who are truly beleaguered and intimidated by the same. Added to this, the social and professional difficulty in collaborating with the younger ones means their cup of woes is full.

A young manager prepared a draft report and sent to his older boss. The moment the report reached the boss, he picked up the phone and asked the manager, 'Do you expect me to read this or leave it in the file?' The young manager thought the boss didn't like the ideas in his proposal. He didn't know what to say. The boss clarified, 'Use large and simple fonts. I find it a struggle to read these.' The young manager was in a dilemma: 'If I upload the file through a web hosting service like Dropbox, he says he is not used to that. He wants me to send files through email. Now he says he has a problem with that also. How can one work in such an environment?'

Here is an interesting incident that happened just when cellphones had made their appearance in the market. A large organization with multiple divisions finally agreed to the request of some young managers for cellphones. The boss of the communication division ordered the cellphones for his managers. However, what he didn't like was the managers carrying a cellphone everywhere, including in the meetings organized by the top bosses. He shouted at them after a meeting, saying, 'Why are you making a "show" of your cellphones in the organization? What would those managers and bosses who did not have cellphones think? Keep the cellphones only in your cabins. Don't display them in public!' The boss could not comprehend the fact that cellphones were meant to be taken along with oneself and not to be kept in one's cabin.

A young manager shared this: 'I am the only daughter of my parents, who stay in our native village. I need to go at least once a month to see them, take them for medical check-ups and attend to other domestic work. Sometimes I club my trip with an official work trip near my native place, but only around a holiday. But my bosses always created hurdles in sanctioning my leave and trips.' She continued, 'This attitude of old bosses stems from a lack of understanding of the situational issues of young persons.'

This is not an isolated case. Times have changed; the structure of family has undergone a change too. Many young officers come from nuclear families. They are equally, if not more, attached to their parents as those of the elder generation. With the collapse of the joint family system, there are no near and dear ones to help them. The bosses who are older have hardly faced such problems. They turn a Nelson's eye to the changing social ethos, giving rise to conflict. To make matters worse, the older bosses, many of whom live in a cocoon, often use the expression, 'You know, in our time...,' a sure dampener on the mood of young managers.

Further, young working parents want to spend quality time with their children. Many older parents didn't think of quality time because they could spare plenty of time for their children. The concept was simply not present. Today, even children are demanding; they expect the presence of their parents at school when they perform or for results. The older managers cannot understand why the young ones are 'making a song and dance' about attending school when their wards perform!

The organization would benefit if a little more empathy is shown to youngsters and their requests are considered more liberally. This is not to say that the older generation managers don't appreciate the sincerity of the younger ones. However, since they have not undergone such issues, there is a gap in understanding. It is also a question of habit; the older generation was not used to applying for leave and often prided themselves on how few leaves they had availed of. Habits die hard and often become ingrained values.

The strains in the digital networking environment

Social networking has brought into the open the inherent differences of the two generations. While the seniors are more sedate and measured in their approach, the younger ones are more open and brazen. Both generations do not relish the vocabulary, tone and gestures of the other. This is evident even more in the digital world. When young officers boldly express their views on online platforms, at times disregarding seniority and protocols, the older people view such activity as rebellious and cheeky. Even techno-savvy seniors feel that mentoring takes a back seat in a virtual environment, and therefore, junior employees should not be allowed to discuss official matters on social networking groups where senior officers may also have a presence. Due to this approach, many young employees avoid having bosses in their circle of friends on social networking sites. There are exceptions, however; instances where very senior employees have taken lessons in social networking from their younger colleagues are also present.

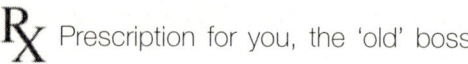
Prescription for you, the 'old' boss

Whether you like it or not, all future-oriented organizations need fresh blood for survival and progress in an environment of rapid changes, competition, diversification and stakeholder expectations. The influx of young managers is inevitable and bosses need to provide them with the best atmosphere possible, to help them contribute their best. The attitudinal, temperamental and behavioural differences between the 'old' and the 'young' in an organization are not deliberate or orchestrated, but a natural outcome of the unique circumstances in which different generations live. Therefore, bosses need to accept the young people as they are and mentor them patiently to respect organizational values and goals.

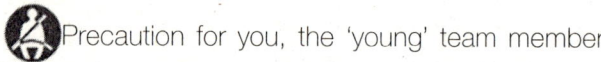
Precaution for you, the 'young' team member

Remember that the organization you are in has been built on the hard work of many, including the present bosses, most of whom joined it while they were young. Though there could be discouraging and disparaging responses from some of the older bosses, rebelling against them will not be the correct solution. You need to understand that the older bosses did not have the opportunity to get exposed to the latest skills and technology like you, and there could be a genuine difficulty in comprehending the rationale behind changes in strategies, processes and outlook desired by you. You need to respect the existing organizational culture and hierarchical relationship structure in your mission to take the organization to a new level. In that process, you might learn a lot from the lessons of the past, which only senior bosses can provide.

Precept for the organization

With the influx of young blood in the organization, it is imperative to prepare and update 'old' seniors, not only about the attitudinal and behavioural orientations of the youngsters, but also of their expectations and capabilities. Appropriate inputs need to be given on the latest managerial strategies, communication tools, and stakeholder expectations. Similarly, young recruits should be given an orientation about the existing organizational culture, challenges successfully tackled by the senior bosses and suggestions to assimilate smoothly and avoid possible confrontation. Such steps can help reduce the gap built on ignorance, prejudices, or false notions about 'who is right' on each issue.

The signs of recovery

Successful organizations ensure that seniors learn and get stimulated by the enthusiasm and creativity of the youngsters, and that youngsters gain from the experience and work culture of the seniors.

22

THE BRAGGARTS

YOU MUST HAVE heard of the Greek mythological hero Narcissus, who fell in love with his own reflection in a pool of water. There are many leaders like him that are in love with themselves. They like compliments, gifts, praise and adoration from the people around them.

A person who indulges in incessant talk about himself, his merits and accomplishments wastes his time as well as the time of the listener. Everyone is allowed to occasionally cast aside modesty and blow their own trumpet to drive home a point or two. However, this should not be done too often.

Someone who worked under a bragger-leader commented: 'I have sympathy for his wife. How could she tolerate his bragging all the time?' To this his colleague remarked, 'It might be quite the opposite. He must be craving for recognition elsewhere.'

The 'I' factor

Professor James W. Pennebaker[62] points out that a person's use of function words such as pronouns, articles, prepositions and conjunctions reveals more about his self. The person who uses 'I' very often in conversation has a strong 'self-focus'. It is natural that people tend to use 'I' more often when they put in more years in their career. This is because they have much to share with others. However, the system will not tolerate overdosage of such wisdom. Further, such frequent references to oneself are not the exclusive preserve of aged bosses; some young leaders can give the elders a run for their money! Ronnie Solan[63] has analysed 'narcissistic self-love' in a very interesting manner, where she reformulated the concept of narcissism as 'not simply a state or trait but the "primary agency" that contains and modulates excitations, functioning as an "immune psychic envelope" of the familiar self'.

Self-admiration is good, but not beyond a point. The popularity of self-admirers is short-lived in any organization. Most of these bosses are not aware of others' reactions to their behavioural patterns; however, some of them may definitely get a clue in the long run. Erika N. Carlson, Simine Vazire and Thomas F. Oltmanns,[64] of the Washington University in St Louis, examined whether narcissists have insight into the negative aspects of their personality and reputation.

They found that narcissists understand that others see them less positively than they see themselves, and they have some insight into the fact that they make positive first impressions that deteriorate over time. Overall, unless bosses understand negative perception early in their career, they may continue to be unpopular.

Acceptable form of bragging

Some organizations believe that a little elaborate detailing of one's achievements in a curriculum vitae (CV) is necessary, and is not bragging. Gone are the days when people provided a very brief biodata to prospective employers. At present, one is given the right to elaborate past accomplishments in the CV. There are many social networking sites like LinkedIn, Myspace, Facebook and Netlog where one can update achievements instantly. Employers and recruiting agents who look for good candidates do not mind going through long CVs, except when they come across 'cut and paste' content. Bragging in a CV or the profile pages of social networking sites becomes unacceptable if they are plain lies.

How much one can indulge in self-promotion?

Boxing champion Muhammed Ali said, 'It's not bragging if you can back it up.' A young consultant who joined one of the big four consulting firms asked, 'Who will promote me other than myself? If I need to be noticed, I need to make myself visible to others. This can happen only through self-promotion since there are very few attractive options and too many people competing for these.'

In his book *Getting Ahead*,[65] author and management consultant Joel A. Garfinkle revealed his signature model for mastering three important skills to reach the top. They are perception, visibility, and influence. According to him, one is required to actively promote oneself as an asset in the organization. For this, one has to make oneself visible to gain the recognition of others. Therefore, one has to adopt a strategy that is not interpreted as bragging, but instead, a sober presentation of one's achievements.

Humility goes before honour

The famous proverb 'Humility goes before honour' is very apt in the area of leadership. Leaders gain respect by being humble. Even if the leader perceives himself as a 'know all' with many achievements to his credit, he should not consider his team members to be mere blockheads. It is necessary that leaders speak as 'we' rather than as 'I'. They need to spend more time listening than speaking.

In a New Year tweet,[66] Clay Christensen, Harvard professor and author of *How Will You Measure Your Life?* said, 'The greatest advice I can give is the greatest advice I've been given: be humble. It has changed me and I think about it every day.'

℞ Prescription for you, the boss

You are superior to your team members in terms of qualification and expertise. That's why you are the boss. However, you don't have to harp on that. Don't try to impress the team with unending narrations of your achievements. Your first impression will quickly change to the worst impression if you continuously self-praise. Allow people in the team to speak about their achievements and compliment them for the same as well.

Precaution for you

Ensure that there is an agenda for meetings and politely remind your boss about the subject for discussion. Respond to the bragging of the boss by gently yet intelligently introducing the main topic.

At times, it may also be better to amuse your boss by acknowledging and appreciating his accomplishments, so that he does not feel the need to narrate them to you too often.

Precept for the organization

Introduce the practice of recording every discussion and meeting, however trivial, and sending the same, along with a summary in the form of minutes, to key functionaries. A replay will help demonstrate how much time has been spent on inconsequential or irrelevant discussions.

If the organization has established appropriate and transparent self-reporting systems where everyone can highlight their achievements, people may not feel the need to indulge in bragging, though some people might still continue to do so.

The signs of recovery

A true leader neither projects himself as overly positive nor encourages praise from others.

23

MR BOSS! DON'T ALWAYS LOOK UP. LOOK DOWN TOO!

WE OFTEN HEAR speakers and life-style gurus talking of gaining inspiration from people who have 'scaled the peak'. We have great leaders, saints, spiritual masters and achievers who can be our role models. However, occasionally we may find such models too idealistic, impractical or out of context.

It is likely that people would not get motivated after repeatedly hearing about the great achievements of role models. We may perceive the great people as endowed with unique virtues, brought up in

unusual circumstances or blessed with infinite potential. As such, we may conclude that they are not ordinary human beings or that their eulogy is too embellished and hard to believe, such that they cannot be easily emulated even though they are worth emulating. Further, we tend to justify the attitude that certain things are impossible for us to do, thus satisfying ourselves with limited achievements and goals.

However, there are several 'ordinary' persons around us and often even below us in a hierarchy from whom we can draw inspiration. It could be our children, employees, servants or other people. When we notice certain achievements or unique traits in them, we may become convinced that great things are achievable by us as well.

Muniraj was the caretaker of a large conference hall in a company where meetings were held almost every day. Most of these meetings went well; there was never really any issue regarding seating arrangements, microphones, projectors or refreshments. No one took note of the service rendered by this one person who did not even take leave for several years. It took a new chief to spot the extraordinary work turned out by this ordinary man; he lost no time in publicly honouring Muniraj. Further, that small gesture didn't go unnoticed: a) Many people realized that they had taken Muniraj for granted and had not noticed his painstaking efforts; b) the senior management realized how spontaneously a leader could communicate with the team and identify committed employees; and c) the whole workforce got motivated by this act. Small actions like these from the boss, in place of long speeches and circulars, can often help galvanize the entire organization.

The following incident was narrated by the CEO of a public sector power infrastructure company. 'A senior advocate of a leading law firm met me to discuss a legal issue my company was facing. After the discussion, we chatted in general about falling efficiency and lack of dedication in the managerial workforce in many public sector organizations. At that point, the elderly lawyer told me about a junior manager in my organization, extolling his wisdom and virtues. What he narrated became a lesson for me: a) the officer was always highly courteous to every visitor, b) he didn't make anyone wait and always strictly adhered to the schedule, c) he came well prepared for meetings and explained things with great clarity, and d) anyone who met him even once would definitely get inspired by his enthusiasm, positive attitude and integrity. He said, "People like him are an asset to your company." I was delighted by this positive feedback about one of our employees and it prompted me to introspect on my own habits and attitudes. What impression do I make on the people I meet? I am not punctual for many of my meetings. I have kept visitors waiting for hours because of poor time management. I have conducted meetings without adequate preparation and consequently, was unclear in my deliberations. I have been short-tempered on many occasions and jumped to conclusions without listening to others. I felt a strong urge to take a leaf out of this young manager's book. Let me share with you that I am grateful to that young man, with whom I have never interacted directly, for showing me how to become a better person and a better boss.'

There are many such ordinary people who can teach us important lessons. A successful person is the one who absorbs the positive traits of others.

Sindhu, while narrating the story of a peon, had this to say, 'The real warriors will always be noticed even if they may never get a chance to make it to the forefront. They are kings and queens of their own world. The most admirable thing about them is their grounded, confident attitude. How I wish the world would stop pretending that only the powerful and "purse-full" people are great!' T.S. Krishnamurthi, former Chief Election Commissioner of India, said in a conversation with me: 'The saying "small minds and great empires would not go together" is absolutely right. It requires a big heart to appreciate the humble creations of God.' Elton Mayo, who led the famous Hawthorne studies, emphasized that respect and recognition from leaders majorly contributes to the performance of workers.

Motivation comes from all around. Sometimes we may not realize how many people or who all have influenced us. But we should realize that the bulk of the credit for our virtues often goes to many ordinary individuals with extraordinary traits.

℞ Prescription for you, the boss

The organization is not just you or your top team. Everyone, from the very top to the very bottom, plays a role in making it the way it is. Your role models need not always be the people above you. There are diamonds below you as well.

 Precaution for you

Modesty is a good attribute. But you should not feel that the work you do is too insignificant and underplay it. That can lead to low self-esteem. The sincerity and commitment you demonstrate could motivate even those who are above you in the organizational hierarchy.

 Precept for the organization

Organizations need to evolve strategies and avenues to recognize and appreciate performers at all levels. It can help bring enthusiasm and motivation that a pay cheque alone does not.

The signs of recovery

Exemplary leaders and effective organizations are always receptive to ideas from everyone, irrespective of their status or rank. Such organizations also know how to acknowledge the contributors appropriately.

Ruth and her new boss

Ruth was always silent during meetings. None of the bosses ever asked for her opinion, since they assumed she didn't have one. She was viewed as reticent, so nothing was discussed with her by colleagues either. Even her juniors often ignored her, thinking that she held no opinion or would not care to divulge her views.

However, though she was an introvert by nature, Ruth was excellent at work. Her new boss, who had joined recently, was an effective communicator; he effortlessly triggered others to open up to him. He found two things lacking in the communication network within the organization. One was the disproportionately high volume of communication from the top with very little feedback from the bottom; this happened at all levels. The second thing was that there were a few blind spots where there were hardly any 'signals' for communication. No one found it necessary to have boosters installed to generate good networks.

Ruth was one such blind spot. Though she was physically present, there was no communication from or to her within the organization. The new boss found that though she was one of the oldest employees in the organization in terms of tenure, she never contributed in discussions and no one sought her opinion. This puzzled the boss, who also found from her personal file that she had been producing outstanding results. The boss called her to his chamber and initiated a very informal chat about her family, interests, hobbies and other details. He found her becoming increasingly forthcoming in her conversation, especially since he also narrated his own interests, family, past career and so on to her. It created a comfortable environment for Ruth, such that the boss could ask her about the activities in the organization, its past and her views on current strategies. He was astonished at what she said. She gave a very objective and succinct appraisal of the organization's past activities as well as clear views on the current strategies and their pros and cons.

The insights shared by Ruth were as good as what the smartest and the most intelligent leaders in the organization had to offer. She was thus an unexplored treasure within the organization. When her views were put across to the top management, all of them were amazed at her knowledge and intelligence.

A good leader is one who facilitates communication flow from the lowest level upwards. He can detect where there is a block; further, he is not satisfied by it being a mere rapid and continuous flow, but will examine whether it is even and inclusive.

24

THE ARCHETYPICAL BOSSES

THERE ARE SEVERAL historic and mythological personalities whose ideas and philosophies live on in individuals today. There are Gandhians, Promethians or Epimethians based on these leaders' personality traits or the behavioural and thought patterns present in people. That is also why we call someone a Stalinist or a Tughlak. In organizations too, we can see leaders who imbibe characteristic traits of certain personalities consciously or unconsciously, where others would attribute some of their unique behavioural patterns as similar to those of someone else.

There are many such 'someone elses' in organizations, who due to their unique traits, leave a legacy. It could be positive or negative. We leave a mark not only on everyone around us, but also historically and geographically. When I say historically, it means that our attitudes, behaviour and personality traits stay recorded in memory for a long period and people tend to talk about these even after we have left the scene. Similarly, the people who reside or relocate to our geographic location may be interested in knowing more about the impressions or impact we have created.

Simon Jos was a studious, bright and clever student. He received gold medals in his graduation and post-graduation. Through hard work, he got into one of the top careers in government service at a very young age, after cracking the country's toughest recruitment examination. As soon as he started on his first posting, some well-wishers advised him: 'Be cautious when making decisions. Wrong decisions could land you in trouble and you might not get promotions on time. With your age, you can easily become the top officer in the country if you get your promotions on time.' This advice 'ruined' his personality over the next few decades.

As the sole aim in Simon's career was to reach the top at any cost, he became extremely cautious in making decisions. What an irony! Though he was selected for the job so that he would take quick decisions, he became the slowest in doing so, and governance was often trapped in red-tape wherever he worked. As time went by and people understood him better, his behavioural pattern became known to his new teams even before he took over any fresh postings. They would say, 'Now we can sleep for three years. This fellow will not do anything progressive or creative in this post.' Years of lethargy, fear and anxiety made him a deadbeat worker in the organization. However, all the promotions he desired came through, such that he reached a stage where he stopped making any decisions whatsoever.

Files piled up in his chamber and he routinely sent them back with irrelevant remarks just to make space for the next load. Simon held the top post for two long years; they were the worst years in the history of that organization. It trailed similar organizations in growth by several years because of him.

What did Simon Jos gain? He gained a title: The deadbeat. He also created a genre of leaders—the 'Simon Jos type boss' where people would say, 'Man, don't be another Simon!' The dominant trait of that person, which Gordon Allport called the cardinal trait, became a permanent hallmark for any person of a similar nature.

According to the trait theory by Allport,[67] there are three broad categories of personality traits. These are the cardinal traits, central (general) traits, and secondary traits. Some people are known for their unique traits which become their signature wherever they go. These are cardinal traits. The person would be known by these traits; many might forget his name but not the characteristic trait that distinguishes him from others. These can be partly influenced by genetic factors. Next, central traits are the ones representing a person's general character and conduct. Examples of this are sincerity, honesty, intelligence, patience and worry. These traits are visible in different situations and yet in exceptional circumstances, these may not be dominant. Lastly, secondary traits are the ones that are not very visible in particular circumstances.

Later, Raymond Cattell identified 16 key personality traits in human beings.[68] However, it was Hans Eysenck[69] who reduced the categorization to three universal traits:

- Introversion/extraversion (people who are reserved/social)
- Neuroticism/emotional stability (people who are emotionally unstable/stable)
- Psychoticism (people with anti-social, hostile and manipulative traits)

A theoretical perspective that synthesizes earlier personality trait categorizations has been formulated mostly in the 1980s by Goldberg[70] and McCrae and Costa.[71] The key traits identified by them based on the conclusions of a few psychologists of the 1960s and 1970s are:

a) Extraversion (sociability)
b) Agreeableness (affection and trust)
c) Conscientiousness (thoughtfulness and systematic)
d) Neuroticism (unstable)
e) Openness (flexibility)

Simon Jos's behavioural pattern can also be observed in several large private sector and public companies. Many senior managers are unconcerned about creating an enduring growth trajectory for the company. Their vision is limited to ensuring a regular revision of their pay and perquisites. Auditors may also not do justice to their role of 'watchdog' if their only aim is to get their fees paid and their contract renewed.

Bosses should be remembered for being the right archetypes and not the toxic ones.

℞ Prescription for you, the boss

Don't think that being a top functionary, your actions and reactions are protected or confidential. There are many who would love to get inputs on every habit and trait, however trivial or routine. Every remark, every word you utter and every gesture you make in confidentiality can be out in no time.

Don't underestimate your subordinates by thinking that they will accept and appreciate your point of view and behaviour. A successful boss is one who understands what his team members want. You should be aware of your shortcomings, weaknesses and inabilities. People below you should respect you not because you are their boss, but because of your unique personality, your efficiency and social traits.

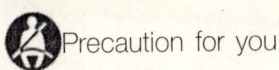

Precaution for you

Know that every action, reaction and even attitude is captured by many people who observe and interact with you every day. This includes not only your creativity, sociability, empathy and unique contributions, but also your idiosyncrasies, weaknesses and mistakes. Therefore, you should put in your best and be aware of your surroundings.

Precept for the organization

Every organization has a culture, value system, strategic goal, and approach that has evolved over time through established rules and conventions, successful practices, and lessons from failed strategies. While incremental or radical changes are welcome from fresh incumbents in top posts if they are seen as beneficial for the organization, no one should be allowed to be dormant or overly hyperactive in implementing strategies according to personal likes and dislikes.

Organizations need to have strict selection criteria for top-level bosses so that people who are neurotic, rigid, manipulative, or opportunistic (to name a few traits) are appropriately assessed and trained, if they have potential, before being selected for a responsible and strategic post or in a job where they need to lead a large team.

The signs of recovery

Enthusiastic leaders spread vigour and vitality around them, and will be remembered for their proactive steps for a long time to come.

25

THE JEALOUS BOSS

WHAT HAPPENS WHEN your boss feels that you're smarter than him? In normal circumstances and for most people, having a smart and efficient subordinate is an asset. In fact, people often want the best picks for their team so that the organization or division produces the best results. However, some bosses perceive this more as a threat than an opportunity. If they feel the employees are more intelligent, competent, or industrious, it can disturb them.

The 'Perumthachan' syndrome

A legend in Malayalam talks about a master carpenter (called 'perumthachan', hence the name of the syndrome) and his son. Raman Perumthachan, the father, was regarded as the reincarnation of the chief architect of the gods, and trained his son Kannan in carpentry skills. In due course, Kannan mastered the art with much more finesse than his father, and became more popular. People began calling the son for complex carpentry tasks instead of the father, which triggered professional jealousy. According to the legend, one day the infuriated father dropped his chisel on his son in the guise of an accident and killed him.

Tom was a senior manager in a large software company in Bangalore (Bengaluru). He had the knack of identifying bottlenecks in a problem and fixing them. He was also very popular in the organization, especially with juniors and freshers. They preferred to approach Tom instead of their own boss whenever they had a problem. It irked the boss that he was not getting due recognition within the company. On the one hand, he was very happy that issues were getting settled faster with Tom's creative involvement. On the other hand, he was jealous of Tom's increasing popularity since he was a subordinate. People used to acknowledge Tom often, whereas the boss felt that he was side-lined by the team.

Tom's boss valued his own ego more than the mileage the company was getting because of his employee. Therefore, at the cost of the company's prospects, he got Tom transferred to another location, but still under his control. He was given a very tough project to manage with the aim of making him fail, so that the news of his failure would be known in the entire company and his popularity would take a hit. However, the reverse happened. Tom gladly took up the tough task as a fresh challenge for him to excel in. He turned around the troubled project such that the company earned 50 per cent more profits than the year before. Unfortunately, a boss is always a boss. Tom's senior hastily recorded poor ratings in the annual appraisal without waiting for the release of annual profit figures, which would have otherwise indicated an excellent performance.

Stars as threats

Why do some bosses consider their star team members to be threats? Is it plain jealousy? Is it a feeling of insecurity and envy? Or is it a tendency to not allow anyone else to take credit for success? In many such instances, one or all of these reasons are the causes for a boss's animosity towards his smart subordinates.

Though the words 'jealousy' and 'envy' are used interchangeably, they have different meanings in the current context. When a boss is aggrieved that he is no longer getting the respect, regard and recognition due to the increasing popularity of another person, and develops negative feelings towards that person, it is described as jealousy. When the boss perceives better capabilities and competencies in another person and desires the same for himself even when he knows he is unable to master those skills, it is called envy. A smart subordinate like Tom invokes both jealousy and envy.

Another young employee shared her experience: 'I was doing

an additional certification sponsored by my organization. My new manager didn't like me pursuing it because she herself didn't have that certification. So she put all types of barriers in my way hoping that I would not do well in the course. She did not realize that by getting the certification I could be better at my job and the company would benefit a lot from that.'

Undoubtedly, professional envy and jealousy on the boss's part are the results of feelings of inadequacy, insecurity, inferiority and ill-will. The last one is distinct from the others. In the first three cases, the boss might be at a perceptibly lower level when certain attributes are compared, resulting in the feelings of inadequacy (unable to be above or at par with the other person), insecurity (because he feels his position is threatened), and inferiority (due to low popularity). Jealousy and envy can happen even when you are superior in knowledge, resources, capability and popularity. In such cases, the reason is ill-will towards the other person: How could they be so popular at their level in the organization?

℞ Prescription for you, the boss

Do not get into a competition mode with your subordinates. Also, try not to perceive a brighter person in the team as a threat to you. Do not reprimand him or her in front of others; instead, you should show appreciation for a bright team member. Look at him or her as a stepping stone for your elevation and an instrument for the growth of the organization.

Further, do not lose confidence, and strive to excel in leadership by providing encouragement and motivation to your team.

Precaution for you

Take deliberate steps to acknowledge your boss, even for the little support you may have received from him. Do not forget to solicit his guidance. Further, do not undermine your boss among colleagues. Instead, talk about his positive traits. Give your boss credit for the achievements of the organization even if he has not contributed much.

Precept for the organization

There should be more than one level of appraisal for a person, such that apart from the immediate boss, appraisals are given by super bosses as well. Feedback from juniors and peers should also be factored in (like a 360-degree feedback).

Signs of recovery

If there is a culture of mutual appreciation and co-operation within the organization, it will become a fertile ground for talent to sprout, spread and fructify.

26

WHEN BOSSES ARE GOOD SLAUGHTERERS

IT WAS GLADSTONE who said that a good leader should be a good butcher. Although authoritarianism was a desirable attribute in older times and conventional leaders, many bosses today continue to have a repressive leadership style, which can have a very negative effect on employees.

Often, the first impression makes the best impression. A senior officer at a public sector bank used to take pride in telling her new team that she was called a 'butcher' by her former team members.

What was the message she was conveying to the team? What was she trying to achieve through her opening gambit? Intimidation, whether done with good intention or bad, will have one fall-out for certain. The boss will have lost the respect of the team.

Many who hold the top position are considered to be slaughterers. They are the smiling or frowning assassins that employees detest. They have a complete stranglehold over their team, and anyone who dares to speak up is mercilessly shown the door. Their position reminds others of Idi Amin, the former President of Uganda, who used to boast, 'I consider myself the most powerful figure in the world.'[72]

An effective leader is one who gets compliance from team members not by issuing threats, but by using his persuasive skills. A slaughterer cannot make his managers go the extra mile.

In the civil services

Authoritarian approaches by leaders are counterproductive and will hinder the creativity of the team. In a recent study conducted by the consultancy firm Head, Heart and Brain, it was found that in the UK, bosses in the civil services are the most threatening ones. Jan Hills, partner at Head, Heart and Brain said that bosses 'are under tremendous pressure to make their organizations leaner, while also improving performance.'[73] In another study,[74] it was reported that many officers in the civil services felt demotivated and planned to quit their jobs because of negative comments about their level of adequacy and efficiency.

A senior officer who had spent more than three decades in the Indian Administrative Service quipped, 'Bosses destroy even the best of the officers with their harsh behaviour.' The stability, security and civility that people expect is not just limited to the civil services. The workplace atmosphere is vitiated by authoritarian bosses. However, discerning leaders can bring smiles back to the workplace!

Use of abusive language by bosses is not uncommon in many organizations. In a case of threatening behaviour by a boss,[75] Australia's Workplace Ombudsman warned that the 'f***' word has no place in the workplace and swearing at staff constitutes bullying. So the boss in question was prosecuted.

A senior lady officer of the Indian civil services shared this: 'I had a horrible boss, a total misogynist, when I was transferred to a faraway state. On my first day at office, I dutifully called on him. I requested him for two days leave to get my daughter admitted into kindergarten. He shouted at me, saying "You have no business asking for leave, look at other officers, they also have young children and they don't ask for leave." I was in tears. He made life hell for me thereafter. And the irony is, I have never asked for special favours because I am a woman. We were living in a guest house, so we needed to hunt for a house, look for a nanny and get my child admitted to school. He refused to see reason. I will never forget his unreasonable attitude. I had to bring my four-year-old child to the workplace and beg my husband to cancel his appointments; we also had to continue living out of suitcases for many days. It hurts even now, after 15 years.'

Do arrogant and repressive bosses have lower intelligence?

Industrial and organizational psychologist, Stanley Silverman, along with a team of scholars at the University of Akron and Michigan State University, has developed a *Workplace Arrogance Scale (WARS)*. According to them, arrogant behaviour of bosses is correlated with lower intelligence scores and lower self-esteem when compared with those who are not arrogant. Further, Dotlich and Cairo (2003)[76] identified 11 behaviours that result in the failure of the organizational leaders. The first one is arrogance; others are melodrama, volatility, excessive caution, habitual distress, aloofness, mischievousness, eccentricity, passive resistance, perfectionism and eagerness to please. Repressive bosses can also be categorized as people with lower social intelligence.

Thus, bosses need to desist from using abusive, sarcastic, and offensive language at work. Arrogant responses from them can indicate their own emotional immaturity and lack of emotional intelligence.

They turn into gentle lambs before their bosses

It is an irony that many horrible bosses are the gentlest and most pleasant ones before their seniors, even if they resent working under them. They may even try to create the impression that they are very placid and considerate towards their own teams. Many employees view this as a ploy to get positive responses from their own bosses.

The need for self-awareness

Do these slaughterers know what others think of them? In an interview, Satya Nadella, the chief of Microsoft, told Adam Bryant of *International New York Times*: 'I do a 360-degree review when hiring personnel. I will ask the individual to tell me what their manager would say about them, what their peers would say about them, what their direct reports would say about them, and in some cases, what their customers or partners may say about them. That particular line of questioning leads into fantastic threads, and I've found that to be a great one for understanding their self-awareness.'[77] The question is, how many bosses really care about what others think about them?

℞ Prescription for you, the boss

Understand that you are going to be very unpopular if you are repressive at work, and most employees would like to have nothing to do with you. Imagine yourself getting ill-treated by an unkind boss and try to change your behaviour.

Precaution for you

You can't do much about an angry and arrogant boss. Politeness and low-key responses may help create a manageable relationship between him and you. However, do not endeavour to emulate him when you become a boss!

Precept for the organization

It is necessary to incorporate tests to check arrogance, rudeness and haughtiness in executives before they are promoted to a senior position, handling a large group of employees.

27

THE BOSS: THE PROFANE SELF AND THE SACRED SELF

REVEREND ANTONY WAS a parish priest in a city church where hundreds of people came for Sunday service and other parish functions. People liked his sermons for his fervency in delivery. 'His prayers touched the soul and he could really make everyone experience the divine', said a young parishioner. However, Reverend Antony was an entirely different person outside church. Those who met him in his office or outside found him to be an 'ordinary' man, cracking low-level jokes, sharing gossip, making shrewd suggestions to get more funds for the church, making critical comments about other priests and people, and so on. In fact, they found his accent, modulation and tone of speech to be totally different from when he was giving a sermon. Of course, one can't crack low-level jokes during a church service. But a few people close to him wondered whether such a sharp contrast was desirable.

Many poets and philosophers from different cultures and regions have opined that social life is a theatre. However, it was Irvin Goffman who operationalized this reality by theorizing and researching on the topic. One can observe similar 'performances' in the leadership environment as well. There is a systematic attempt to showcase behaviour that impresses others on formal occasions, but in the 'back stage', a completely different pattern emerges. Many leaders try to indulge in contrasting back stage and front stage performances in the process of 'impression management', a term coined by Goffman.

The above patterns can also be examined from the sacred–profane dichotomy, which was originally propounded by classical French sociologist Emile Durkheim in the context of the sociology of religion. In his theory, 'sacred' represented the interests of the group that are embodied in formal symbolism, whereas the 'profane' represented mundane individual concerns. An ideal leader has to necessarily showcase the best dimensions of his personality to the team and others. But he may not be a perfect person; he would have his own mundane interests and commitments.

There are bosses in many organizations who behave like Reverend Antony. They maintain a high standard in speech, conduct and facial expressions and when airing their views while they are in office, but speak and behave in an entirely different manner in informal meetings outside of work. Even their most ardent fans would view such behaviour distastefully. Their employees may also get confused and want the real boss to stand up. Why do bosses have two sets of behaviour? Do they believe they can earn the respect of their employees that way?

There could be an argument justifying behavioural inconsistencies at work and informal settings. Even in the latter environment, where a boss meets the employees at say, his residence, he need not be his formal self. But to what extent can bosses indulge in random conversations, jokes and worthless gossip? There are a few bosses who would announce in such selective gatherings that people need not take his comments in the meeting at office seriously, as it was done for the official records! Though this can soothe those who feel ruffled by the remarks in the official meeting, such bosses really cut off the branch they are sitting on.

Nausheen shared her experience with a boss who always spoke about fairness and honesty in meetings: 'My team leader, who was an utterly audacious lady, was getting undue advantage over all of us because of her closeness to the boss. I happened to confront her for deviating from company rules, which became a big issue with a lot of shouting and swearing. I received a warning from my company for not behaving professionally and after a month I was removed from the project, while she, a second-level manager, was offered a permanent position, defying all clauses of contract.'

Role conflicts or deliberate behaviour?

There are situations where leaders face an intense role conflict when they are posted to jobs that are not tailor-made for them. If a casual manager is put in charge of disciplining and supervising interns, he will definitely try to put on a different 'self' while he is with the interns. This behavioural mismatch can in turn affect the juniors. If a boss deliberately behaves as a disciplined and systematic person even when he is not disciplined in his own work or is disorganized in his official activities, he would not get accepted by those around him. Certain standards of behavioural consistency are expected from leaders at every level.

℞ Prescription for you, the boss

You can't keep changing your character and conduct, although you could follow a different style in each role.

Precaution for you

You should not be continuously in judging mode. If your boss talks and behaves as he is expected to in the organization, you need not be bothered about how he behaves outside. It is useless to harbour a cynical attitude towards his actions, utterances and inconsistencies.

Precept for the organization

Though organizations cannot keep bosses under surveillance all the time, it can identify the behavioural aberrations that are very apparent and detrimental to the organization and take corrective action.

The signs of recovery

When the boss shows behavioural consistency irrespective of the environment he is in, he will be rated as honest and trustworthy.

28

THE BOSS BY DEFAULT

THE CREDIBILITY AND acceptability of a boss greatly influences the performance and commitment of his team. It is not just legitimacy of the appointment that the team will look for, but also the suitability of the incumbent. Some examples of 'bosses by default' are those who are appointed by virtue of consanguinity, seniority or as part of a standby arrangement.

Boss by virtue of consanguinity

Many large companies all over the world are family-owned or family-managed, while others are under the control of a handful of families. Succession is a crucial process in all such businesses. The first challenge of any large family-run organization during succession planning is that either there are too many contenders to step into the shoes of the boss or there is no one competent enough to take charge.

In many cases, people are appointed to leadership positions simply based on consanguinity rather than professional expertise or competence. Managers below them might thus find it difficult to adjust to these bosses who may hardly know anything about the internal dynamics of the workplace or its unique culture. One may argue that there is lateral recruitment at very senior levels for most big companies and things work well there. However, the people selected to head those companies are ones who have demonstrated their expertise in similar areas of business before. In the case of family-run companies, when the appointments are made purely on the basis of family ties so that familial control is intact, this model may not work.

There are some advantages of having bosses who have acquired positions solely on the basis of lineage. They are invariably loyal to the organization and may have a sense of commitment to protect its wealth and reputation. However, the main disadvantage is that the organization, by not attracting talent from outside, may become relatively stagnant if the incumbents are not ready to innovate.

There is a Lancashire proverb that says clogs to clogs is only three generations. The meaning comes close to: family-owned businesses will be in shambles by the time the founders' grandchildren take charge of them. When employees work under bosses who neither share the vision of the predecessors nor appreciate the strategic plans and commitment of the key managers, there will be overall dissatisfaction and frustration; the company can even begin to go downhill.

Boss by virtue of seniority

It is unfortunate that seniority is valued more than competence in many organizations. Though it was thought that the seniority rule is applicable only in government and public sectors, there are many organizations in the private sector that prefer to promote those who have longer years of experience to important positions.

Selecting someone on the basis of seniority undoubtedly results in a competitive disadvantage for any organization. However, that is the easiest option for the organization to promote the person; it is also an admission of the faulty performance appraisal and management system in many organizations. The advantages of the rule of seniority are: there is no favouritism, there is predictability of prospects, it is more popular among employees because it's an easy route to go on, and there is less dissent within the organization. At the same time, the disadvantages outweigh the advantages of the rule of seniority: there is no motivation to perform, incompetent people are elevated, there is lack of competitive advantage, there is reduction in fresh intake after some levels, innovation gets affected, and so on. The practice followed in the armed forces in many countries is worth emulating. All senior positions in these military establishments are based on merit as well as seniority.

Appointments solely based on the criterion of seniority would thus lead to inefficiencies at the top. Young managers would not like to work under very old seniors who cling to outdated strategies. Annual appraisals become a meaningless exercise if more weight is given to the number of years one has put in. The famous Peter Principle that 'managers rise to the level of their incompetence' is very apt in this context.

Other instances

Other instances of 'boss by default' include appointing someone on an *ad hoc* basis when the first boss leaves or is asked to do so. Often, such standby arrangements continue for longer than necessary. In such scenarios, the organization can be at a disadvantage and the team may have a lack of direction.

Prescription for you, the boss

You may not be in a top post by merit, but you could show others that you deserve that position through your actions. By conceiving and pursuing systematic and deliberate steps to learn something new such that you take the organization to higher level, as well as promoting the creative ideas of people below you in the organization, you can ensure credibility and acceptability at the workplace.

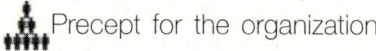Precaution for you

Watching how the 'boss by default' works, envying his glory or criticizing him is not going to lead anywhere positive. The bosses are there based on certain established conventions. You should be wise enough to support the boss by contributing your best rather than taking a cynical backseat.

Precept for the organization

Credibility of the 'bosses by default' can be boosted through well laid out strategies. Family businesses need to invest in leadership development within. Even when an insider is appointed to a position in top management, it should be done by following certain best practices that are fair, rational and transparent.

In organizations that fill top positions on the basis of seniority, there needs to be a criterion that considers performance as well during the decision-making process. This will ensure fairness in appointments and competence at higher levels and will also boost the morale of the teams.

The signs of recovery

When the job is performed with seriousness and commitment, and a climate of trust and open communication with the management team is created, apprehensions and cynicisms against a 'boss by default' would disappear.

29

THE PATHETIC APATHETIC BOSS!

RALPH WALDO EMERSON said, 'Nothing great was ever achieved without enthusiasm'. Only an enthusiastic leader can nurture an enthusiastic team. A lazy, droopy boss can kill vigour and make his team deadbeat.

'Enthusiasm is the sparkle in your eyes, the swing in your gait. The grip in your hand, the irresistible surge of will and the energy to

execute your ideas', said Henry Ford, who created history through his enthusiastic endeavours. No one can be in an upswing mood 24×7, but neither should one be downcast or in dull spirits all the time.

There is a tendency of thinking 'Why should I care?' and 'How does it matter to me?' among many bosses. 'Work to Rule' personalities might save their skin, but they are not necessarily effective individuals. They lack concern, are impassive and can be very pessimistic at times. It is difficult for such persons or even those around them to be creative.

Using a company-based data set on the productivity of workers, supervisory effects were estimated by Lazear, Shaw and Stanton where they found that the kind of boss and the productivity of workers is directly related. They also found that an efficient organization allocates the better bosses to the better workers because such bosses increase the productivity of high-quality workers more than that of low-quality workers.[78] One need not be hyperactive or hypervigilant but they can be what Morten T. Hansen of the University of California called 'the ability of productive paranoia'.[79]

The pathetic apathetic boss! § 133

The aversion to providing immediate attention

Tomorrow….tomorrow… that never comes! One of the common habits that makes bosses ineffective is procrastination. With apathetic bosses, delaying tactics are often coupled with laziness to be creative. Postponing work without any valid reason can only make the task more burdensome and uninteresting. Procrastination due to a boss's indecisive nature is also damaging because it not only delays the tasks on hand, but also blocks the possibility of alternatives. The best method to get over procrastination is to do the difficult or uninteresting tasks first.

The boss who is in a state of 'nirvana'

Enthusiasm, vigour and dynamism are the hallmarks of a person who leads an organization that is expected to be continuously innovative and improving, in order to survive in a competitive environment. The leader should be receptive to new ideas, provide opportunities for people to innovate and be willing to discard those aspects of the organization that need to be replaced.

Mr Shom was an active leader during the earlier years of his career. He was known for implementing many innovative projects in the organization. However, after working for more than two decades, some of the 'fizz' had evaporated. He was not the same leader who bubbled with enthusiasm and sparkled with new ideas. He started telling his subordinates, 'One needs to slow down. Why the hurry? Why start a new process?' Thus, his thoughts and ideas were not in tune with the strategies necessary in a result-oriented organization.

A successful organization is one that reinvents itself. It is constant in its commitment to innovate and is consistent in implementing new ideas across all areas of operation. However, people like Shom, due to changes in personal preferences, lifestyle, or attitudes, start having a different approach to the way the organization should function. Transformation in personal life may impact their nature and extent of involvement in the organization. Minor lifestyle modifications, attitudes, behavioural patterns, and so on are natural and can be accepted as normal in any organization. However, the situation becomes abnormal when radical changes in personal priorities adversely affect the performance of the person at the workplace.

'Ashramas' style of leadership transitions

According to Hindu philosophy, there are four stages (or ashramas) in life. They are brahmacharya,[80] grahastha,[81] vanaprastha[82] and sanyasa.[83] During brahamacharya, an individual equips himself with educational and professional skills. In grahastha, he indulges himself in the material world. In the third stage, he is on a mission to understand the depth of life; this is also a time for introspection unbridled by the circumstances he is in. In the last stage, he enters sanyasa, where he renounces the world, realizing the futility of worldly life.

Stages similar to the 'ashramas' can be seen in the professional lives of many people. Often, those who spend their lifetime in a single organization undergo a lifecycle change in their career. However, this type of leadership evolution can be detrimental to the well-being of an organization. The 'ashramas' type of leadership transitions can be represented as given below:

Ashramas	Stage in career	The nature of involvement
Brahmacharya	Period of training, probation, enthusiastic learning; immediate implementation of ideas	Urge to learn and excel; being frank and forthcoming
Grahastha	Reaching a confidence level, enjoying the associated perks and privileges, being ambitious, furthering strategies for growth	Encouraging and experimenting with creativity; responsibly fulfilling the leadership role; planning and suggesting innovation

Vanaprastha	Feelings of dissatisfaction and frustration; slowly drifting away from core work; becoming cynical about processes; trying to escape from routine work	Not feeling independent; not being heard; exploring an escape route
Sanyasa	Understands the futility of confrontation; is totally complacent about the way things proceed; advocates moderation at all levels and areas; becomes philosophical or withdrawn.	In a blissful retirement mood; 'let it be' attitude with no worries; tolerates deviants and forgives traitors; attends to mundane tasks only

There are many bosses who go into a stage of 'sanyasa' during their career. A work environment with an apathetic boss can dampen the spirits of the entire team and impact overall employee engagement. In a survey[84] conducted by Dale Carnegie Training along with MSW Research, it was found that the member's relationship with the immediate supervisor is one of the key drivers of employee engagement.

It is said that the life of an individual is like that of the sun. It rises at dawn and as the day progresses, it starts radiating heat and light till it reaches maximum intensity by afternoon. Later it goes down, radiating less heat and light. By evening, it sinks below the horizon before it disappears. Apathetic and sleepy bosses are like the sun at dusk. They are responsible for a dull team at work. As observed in the Hawthorne studies, 'they turned the lights up, productivity improved; they turned the lights down, same thing'. What the team wanted from the management was attention rather than neglect.

℞ Prescription for you, the boss

Do not let your 'nirvana' state pull down the results of your organization. Rejuvenate yourself by updating your skills in a dynamic academic and professional environment, get exposed to new best practices that can be emulated within your organization or take a temporary break from work. If none of these are interesting or nothing works, then take permanent 'nirvana' from work instead of doing a shoddy job.

Precaution for you

You can't really do much about this. Also, if your boss is incorrigibly laid back, then your overenthusiasm might not be palatable to him. However, that does not mean you also follow the boss's path.

You can decide to quit the job if you also get into a 'sanyasa' mode that hinders your performance as well as that of the organization.

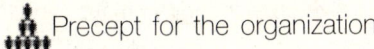Precept for the organization

The first responsibility for an apathetic boss should be with the organization. If top bosses are laid back, the organization can go into a decline. The HR division needs to give their first boosters to such bosses to make them enthusiastic, creative and dynamic before looking at the people below.

The signs of recovery

The boss who follows the above prescription would look at the organization with a new perspective. The team members would also feel invigorated in such an environment.

30

WHEN THE BOSS BECOMES A CEO: THE CHIEF EGO OFFICER

THERE WAS A mandatory 'open session' convened by the big boss of a multinational company to meet employees and hear about their grievances and suggestions. In his opening remarks, he asked them to share their issues frankly without any hesitation. Not many were forthcoming. The super boss told the employees that the success of the company was everybody's responsibility, and they should give their feedback. After a few moments of silence, one manager spoke about certain difficulties and failures in the project. He said, 'Had my proposals for changing the design been approved by my boss, the company would not have faced the crisis at the end.' Immediately, everyone looked at his boss, whose expression betrayed his egotist behaviour. His face had reddened, and he looked as if he was thinking about how his junior could dare talk against his boss to the super boss! That was the last time any employee aired an opinion in the sessions. The scheme of having open sessions closed shortly thereafter and the employee who shared the feedback got his worst ever year-end rating in his appraisal.

There are many bosses who do not want team members to interact directly with the super bosses, even in an informal environment. For example, the boss of a pharmaceutical company always ensured that the top management was seated in a separate enclosure, away from other senior team members in the organization, during official parties.

A senior manager of a software company said, 'There was a high-profile project that I was leading. I ensured that I informed my boss about the challenges and their effect on the timeline. He completely ignored the same even though I reminded him umpteen times; he was not willing to listen as it was coming from a junior. When the project reached a stage of implementation, the glitches mentioned by me emerged, and my boss blamed me for them. It was found to be a case of mismanagement and then shifting the blame to someone else.'

Leaders who have a large number of people working under them may sometimes develop an inflated ego and become reluctant to take advice or suggestions. They become averse to negative feedback and only encourage those who praise them. They give an impression that those who are unhappy with their style can leave the organization. Leaders should keep their ears to the ground so that they become the first to know of a new idea. However, egotist leaders who are preoccupied with themselves or their own ideas are often oblivious to the talents of juniors.

Some egotists deceive people by putting on a show of being humble and simple. However, in reality they not only expect adoration and admiration, but also believe in their right to be pampered.

This is a good joke shared by a friend, about a smart youngster who wanted to get away from such a boss. The boss was in an expansive mood after lunch one day and invited his personal staff to listen to a couple of jokes. Everybody, except one girl, laughed at the not-so-humorous jokes just to impress him. 'What is the matter?', the boss asked the young girl, 'Haven't you got a sense of humour?' The girl immediately said, 'I don't have to laugh. I am leaving this Friday, anyway.'

Some ways in which typical egoistic bosses behave are as follows:

- Make it a point to make the team wait for their arrival in meetings
- Blame others when there is a failure or mistake
- Promote those who praise them
- Get emotional when there is dissent
- Do not attempt to learn as they believe there is nothing they don't know
- Are reluctant to collaborate with others out of the fear that they will have to share the credit
- Want to be in the public spotlight and are worried about negative reporting
- Are conscious about maintaining and boosting their image and take deliberate attempts to work on it
- Like efficiency but not efficient persons, especially if they try to project themselves
- Snub suggestions from others in meetings

Egotism is worse than egoism

Though used interchangeably, 'egotism' refers to a behavioural pattern stemming from the feeling of superiority over others, whereas 'egoism' refers to a belief that actions are motivated by self-interest.

In its positive sense, the 'ego' is an important part of one's personality. As propounded by Freud, there is conscious awareness in every person, which is nothing but ego. It contains within itself judgement, tolerance, perception of reality, sensible justifications, exercise of control, planning, analysis and synthesis of facts. In the negative realm, the ego encapsulates rationalization of one's actions based on subjective conclusions, denial, projection of one's self and an inflated perception of one's capability. When we discuss the ego of the boss, what we discuss here is the negative connotations as understood in modern organizational settings.

Egotistic behaviour has led to the career demise of many bosses. People who pampered their egos beyond a manageable limit have lost their positions over time. Having an ego is not bad if it contributes to boosting self-confidence and enhancing the boss's courage to lead the organization, even in troubled times.

℞ Prescription for you, the boss

You need to examine why people do not come to you with a feedback or suggestions. If most people in your team simply nod in agreement and praise your work regularly, don't get carried away.

A successful boss is the one who does not get trapped by self-pride and ego. He is receptive to the ideas and opinions of everyone below even though he does not follow every suggestion. He respects and values the views of the members.

You should not be reluctant to come out of your ivory tower and meet and interact with the team. Be aware that egotistic leaders are the least respected and the most unpopular in any organization. The only gain is that you satisfy your own self. Instead of the ego controlling you, you should channelize the ego to help provide stable and strong leadership.

Precautions for you

Be tactful while suggesting ideas or pointing out mistakes to egotist bosses. Do this in a private meeting with the boss; egotist bosses can react sharply in a group. Further, present disagreements in a gentle manner by giving a host of reasons that do not directly point out his failure.

Understand that even egotist bosses clearly know who is efficient and appreciate them privately.

Precepts for the organization

Bosses with fragile egos invariably kill the vibrancy and vitality of the team. Identify such people and assess the extent of damage caused by them. If they are unmanageable, shift them to divisions where they cause the least damage.

Understand and empathize with the people who suffer under egotistic bosses and support them by giving them an alternate work environment that is conducive to efficient work.

The signs of recovery

When the boss starts interacting with his team at all levels and makes deliberate efforts to listen to what they have to say, he will be able to understand the path he and the organization need to take. Communication is key to shedding one's inflated ego.

How much does your boss know you?

It is said that the reason for Emperor Napoleon III's success was his ability to remember the names of most of the people he had met. He used to write down their names when no one was looking. 'Look! He remembered me by name!', people used to be surprised when they were called by name by him.

Take the following test to check how much your present boss (or any earlier boss) knows you

Exercise 1.1 (Circle your answer)

No.	Question	Yes	No	I don't know	Total score
1	Does your boss know your full name?	1	0	0	
2	Does your boss know your birth date?	1	0	0	
3	Does your boss know where you stay?	1	0	0	
4	Does your boss know about your family?	1	0	0	
5	Does your boss know who your parents are?	1	0	0	
6	Does your boss know of your past achievements?	1	0	0	
7	Does your boss know how you travel to office?	1	0	0	
8	Does your boss know your educational qualifications?	1	0	0	
9	Does your boss know your hobbies and interests?	1	0	0	
10	Does your boss know about your medical history/health status?	1	0	0	
	Score				

Now, take the test given on the next page to check how much you know about people working under you and those one level under them

Exercise 1.2

No.	Question	Yes All	Yes Most	Very few	Total score
1	Do you know the full names, with correct spellings, of all the persons directly reporting to you?	2	1	0	
2	Do you know the names of all the persons working one level below those directly under you?	2	1	0	
3	Do you know how many children each person working under you has?	2	1	0	
4	Do you know where the people working directly under you stay?	2	1	0	
5	Do you know the educational qualifications of all the persons working under you?	2	1	0	
6	Do you know the health conditions of the people directly working under you?	2	1	0	
7	Do you know how the persons directly working under you travel to office?	2	1	0	
8	Do you know about the hobbies or interests of the persons working under you?	2	1	0	

9	Do you know the dietary habits of the persons directly working under you (are they vegetarian or non-vegetarian)?	2	1	0	
10	Do you know about the health conditions of the parents or family members of the persons directly working under you?	2	1	0	
	Score				

Go to page 255 for analysis of your score

31

THE BOSS AND YOUR HEALTH

FAISAL WAS WORKING in a transnational cargo company. One day, he felt exhausted at work and informed his colleagues that he had mild chest pain. Within minutes, he collapsed at his desk. He was quickly shifted to a hospital, where the doctor diagnosed a mild cardiac attack. When his HR manager visited him a few days later to enquire about his welfare, Faisal requested only one thing: 'I need a change from the present office.' His request was acceded to. A year later, when his former colleagues visited him at the new office, they had a pleasant surprise. The man who had always been worried earlier had become an enthusiastic and pleasant person. Even his style of dressing and grooming had improved. When asked for the reason, he said, 'Once I left that cranky boss, my health started improving. My doctor says I don't require medicine any more, which I had been taking all those years under the old boss. My new boss is my inspiration. I have started playing tennis, joined a new course, exceeded my targets at work, and I spend more time with my family.'

After studying the health status of about 3000 employees over a period of 10 years, a group of Swedish researchers[85] found that having terrible bosses (according to employees) increased the risk of heart disease by 25 per cent. It was found that the longer the employees worked for a bad boss, the worse their health condition became. Those who worked for more than four years with a bad boss had a 64 per cent higher risk of heart disease.

Many organizations check the health status of a candidate before appointing them. Some continue to examine their fitness at regular intervals; this is not only aimed at the welfare of the employees, but also to protect the interest of the organization. Many governments have initiated the process of annual medical check-ups along with appraisals. It is necessary that organizations that have genuine concern for the welfare of their employees analyse data collected over a period of time and examine how the work culture and working conditions are impacting employee health.

It is said that people waste more than 20 hours a week worrying about their bosses and their responses. McQuaid[86] found that about 70 per cent of people said they would have been happier at work if they got along better with their boss, with the breakdown equal amongst men and women; however, younger workers in their 20s and 30s skewed even higher (80 per cent). Quoting various research studies, Robert Sutton[87] has said that those with good bosses lead a less stressful life and have fewer heart ailments. According to him, 75 per cent of the workforce feels that their immediate boss is the most stressful part of their work environment.

Studies have thus shown that the well-being of employees strongly depends on the nature of organizational support and the interpersonal style of bosses.[88] Psychologist Robert Hogan, who has studied this subject extensively,[89] noted that bad managers are a major health hazard and impose huge medical costs for individuals and organizations. Further, the American Psychological Association found in a study[90] that 69 per cent of employees in their sample reported that the job is a significant source of stress. An executive in a large software company told me that once a week, he and his friends sat over beer and snacks just to share their negative experiences with bosses. He observed that these get-togethers helped them de-stress.

Governments all over the world have established healthcare legislations to be enforced at work. These legislations focus on the conditions of health, hygiene, sanitation, safety and so on in organizations. One important element that has not been factored in is boss-centred stress. Studies mentioned here reveal that most of the health problems of employees in modern organizations are not related to just the work conditions referred to above, but also the strain caused by the attitudes and behaviour of bosses.

In a study conducted by Marilyn Macik-frey et al.,[91] it was found that authentic leaders provide a supportive and positive environment where a positive mood is nurtured in the organization. According to them, these transformational behaviours can also be conceptualized as a health-promoting strategy among employees. Most employees spend more hours at work than with their families. Undoubtedly then, health is wealth and it is important for companies to ensure that positive health conditions exist in the workplace.

Prescription for you, the boss

Just because someone is working under you does not mean that his life is under your control and you can behave any way you wish. A team member will put his best foot forward only when he is convinced of the importance of the task and is treated with trust, respect, fairness and recognition by his immediate boss. In the best interest of the organization, you must also ensure that team members have enough time to relax and rejuvenate in a manner they like, rather than making them undergo a structured relaxation schedule.

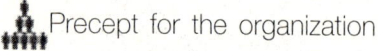
Precaution for you

A highly stressed environment in office is detrimental to one's health. Make sure you understand that life is not your career alone. Your life should decide your career and not the other way around. Your commitment, hard work, and creativity at work should not affect your or your family's happiness, peace and health.

Precept for the organization

Organizations should ensure that employees get to work in a stress-free environment. Independent and confidential channels should be in place, where employees can share their feedback about the attitudes and behaviour of bosses as well as report stress contributors in office.

Annual health check-ups should be used as a tool to analyse the physical and mental status of employees. Immediate corrective action should be taken for reducing stress if present; these can include job rotation, transfer of place or position, moving the boss, counselling and medical assistance.

Bosses who are branded as stress creators by employees should be trained or moved to appropriate alternate roles.

The signs of recovery

Good bosses can bring about wonders in the organization. A person who is happy at work also brings happiness to his family.

> **Questions to ponder and introspect on**
>
> Most of us spend the best part of our lives working in organizations for our livelihood. Medical experts say that our health status is directly related to our lifestyle, nature of activities, attitudes and experiences. Therefore, our professional life has a definite bearing on our health. In the previous chapter we saw how the boss's nature influences the personal lives of people working under him. It is clear that a stressful boss can affect one's health. At the same time, one can get rejuvenated by association with a caring boss.
> Do you think you've suffered from adverse health conditions because of the stress created by a boss?
> Do you think your team members are relaxed when working under you?
> Are you flexible enough to revise targets or reduce expectations when you find that a team member is stressed out?
> Have you made people work more than they are supposed to because others are not capable?

32

BOSSING AFTER BOSSING HOURS

NANCY WAS WORKING with a leading airline company as its relationship manager, and was in charge of high-valued clients. She thoroughly enjoyed working and won the 'Best Employee Award' many times. Once its travel business became fully online, the company allowed its executives flexible hours so that they could work from home for two days in a week. Many thought it was a boon. But for Nancy, it was a nightmare. She had to be online attending tasks not just those two days in a week, but every day after office hours and also on holidays. Often, she had to leave guests at dinner to attend online calls. Even family outings and movies were interrupted, much to the annoyance of her family members. She would also get calls from clients to reschedule flights or allow late

check-ins. She finally quit the job after getting fed up with 'off-office working', and started looking for a normal 10 to 5 job where no one would disturb her beyond office hours.

In a study conducted with about 600 employees in the US and Canada, it was found that 40 per cent of employees feel harassed because of emails received from their bosses on weekends and holidays.[92] Though electronic communication has made life a little easier, it has also thrown up fresh challenges around time boundaries, such that employees are often asked to respond to mails instantly from their smart phones. As such, they have to be available literally 24×7.

A middle-level manager at a public sector company told me, 'My previous boss used to like having discussions only in the evenings, when I was about to leave, even for matters that could easily wait till the next day. He wasn't in any hurry to get back to his family and didn't realize my need to spend time with mine. I was very relieved when I secured a transfer to another division.'

Mobile connections are taken as a corporate package for optimizing bills and to get a common number series by many organizations. However, this has become a bane for many employees. They are asked to respond to official calls beyond office hours and even on holidays. According to one employee who works in a private sector enterprise, if calls were not answered, especially those received at night, her boss would shout at her. She said, 'I need private space in my life. I don't want to get disturbed when I am at home, just because the mobile connection is an official one.' Recently, Germany's employment ministry banned its managers from calling or mailing staff out of office hours unless there was an emergency.[93]

Sharma, one of the top bosses of a large organization, is on the verge of retirement. He comes late to office and stays till late at night for work. He even expects everyone below him to stay in office till he leaves. Most meetings are fixed in the late evening and he often wastes time with unnecessary chats. This has created difficulties for the managers with young children. However, Sharma is not bothered about inconveniences created for others due to his irregular work schedule.

Intrusion into personal lives

It is good to see bosses showing an interest in the personal lives of their team members; it is an important attribute of successful bosses. However, if this interest and involvement becomes excessive or amounts to interference in personal matters and invasion of privacy, then it will be resisted. There are bosses who think they are best suited to give advice to subordinates on all matters—whether official or private.

Saxena's children hated their father's boss. He would call home very often late in the evenings and engage in long conversations with their father. This was the time they interacted with their father for general chatting, watching TV together, and doing homework. However, calls from the boss would disturb such plans. Mrs Saxena also disliked these calls because they disturbed her schedule for shopping, dining out, movies and general time with her husband. What they disliked even more was the series of suggestions given by the boss to Saxena on what they should do, which school the children should attend, which investment is appropriate for the family, and so on.

Bosses who take an extra interest in the personal lives of employees are not very common in western countries. In countries like India, however, some bosses behave as if the employees are bonded labourers and work can be demanded from them any time, including on holidays. They advocate a work culture that demands undivided attention to one's job and argue that family priorities need to take a backseat for the sake of the career.

℞ Prescription for you, the boss

Don't get carried away by the respect and regard you are getting at work from team members. You must understand that they need their personal and family space. Unless it is unavoidable, you should desist from the practice of monitoring work or making work-related requests after office hours. Don't expect them to be available and accessible all the time.

 Precaution for you

Sincerity towards work and respecting the bosses are good virtues. However, you should be able to distinguish between genuine needs and sheer exploitation. You should not feel reluctant to express personal inconveniences to bosses who are in the habit of disturbing you after work hours.

 Precept for the organization

Organizations should frame and implement a policy that stipulates a 'Do not call registry' where employees can communicate if they do not wish to receive calls beyond office hours.

It is also appropriate to record the reasons for making people work beyond office hours by the respective bosses.

The signs of recovery

Organizations with a good work culture and high ethical standards do not need to extract personal time from employees for their benefit.

33

APPRAISAL: THE BOSS'S AMMUNITION AND THE SUBORDINATE'S NIGHTMARE

I HEARD SOMEONE say jokingly, 'In my organization no good work goes unpunished.' This comment points to a larger issue in the system of appraisal within organizations. Evaluation of performance is an absolutely essential process in Human Resource Management. The fundamental purpose of appraisal is to assess the performance of a person and appropriately reward or reform them; it is not a tool to reprimand or punish. The performance appraisal system has been renamed as performance management system globally by many organizations to underline its objective of streamlining performances within a system and ensuring equilibrium in the same. In this system, the emphasis is on reallocation of responsibilities based on past performance, such that there is optimal balance between the nature of tasks and the person responsible for them.

A lot of ill will and relationship issues occur in organizations on account of a perception that the appraisals were unfair. There are many instances of protracted disputes on poor ratings in performance reports, both in public and private sectors.

Mr Mehta works for a large government organization, and said, 'A few bosses are cowards and back stabbers. They give a rating "good" instead of "very good" or "outstanding" in annual appraisals knowing that such reports are buried for a long time without the employee ever knowing that.' This was in the context of an organization where procedures earlier stipulated that if the boss gave an 'adverse' rating then only it had to be communicated to the employee, so as to give the latter an opportunity to file an appeal. The rating 'good' was considered not adequate and the employee would not be informed about it. Mehta, who is still in the organization, said, 'Fortunately, they have removed this unfair appraisal system recently.'

Some of the views shared by managers in the private sector are:

- In some companies, ratings are given before results are out, so good performers are often at a disadvantage. The appeal processes are not smooth, especially when the manager above does not support them.
- Appraisals in the offices of some MNCs are not consistent. They have different evaluation parameters for employees working in different countries.
- HR is weak in many companies. There is dual responsibility for managers (project and HR), so there can be biases in performance appraisal.

There are many bosses who are stingy about giving a good rating in appraisals, but expect an excellent rating from their bosses. A smart super boss asked the boss, 'If you have rated all 10 managers under you less than three out of five, I should take an average of that and give you also less than three. If none of your managers has performed well according to your analysis, that means you have not done your duty well. I should, in fact, give you less than two.' From that day, the strategy changed. The boss started giving outstanding ratings to the managers below so that he could get a similar, if not greater, rating from his boss.

In many organizations, appraisals do not have any value unless there is an adverse rating. This is because no extra incentive or recognition is given even if someone has performed exceptionally well. Promotions are given based on seniority. Only if someone gets a very poor rating are his promotion chances affected, and that too only till the disposal of review applications or appeals, if any.

There are two extreme categories of appraisal writers who are dangerous. The first is 'nasty bosses' who give poor appraisals to almost everyone under them because they think no one can match their efficiency or standards. The second category is 'please-all' bosses who give excellent ratings to all under them. They encourage underperformers and disappoint good performers through this unfair judgement.

Why do people perceive an appraisal as faulty?

- Performance is not accurately measured
- Performance expectations are not clear
- Matching resources are not provided
- Certain areas of work are not factored into the appraisal system
- Weight for different parameters is given wrongly
- Grading parameters are not communicated in advance
- Everyone gets a good rating irrespective of contribution
- Everyone gets an adverse rating irrespective of performance
- The appraisal is done by someone who has supervised work only for a small part of the process

Why do employees accuse an appraisal as unfair?

- Performance targets are unachievable
- Performance targets are inequitable
- Performance standards were not communicated
- There is no interim feedback on performance during the task period
- Little or no opportunity is given for self-appraisal
- No pre-appraisal discussion is conducted
- Requested resources that are essential for performance are not provided

Why are some employees not scared of appraisals?

- They are about to retire
- The organization does not take any action on good or bad reports
- The member feels that his super boss would overrule the adverse report of the immediate boss
- The member has already negotiated for a better assignment or post outside the company
- The member has enough financial security to fall back on even if the appraisal affects his position or remuneration
- The employee considers his boss unworthy of evaluating his performance
- The person has already got an assured elevation in the organization
- He doesn't believe in or care about appraisals and is ready to face the consequences

When the appraisal is very 'personal'

John shared his experience with a boss in his company, EBM India: 'One day, during training, a senior boss asked me to do something out of the way as a favour for a new recruit, a girl with connections to the then head of the company. He said he would give me more details later. I did not hear from him after that. I did not follow through on the favour, because I did not feel comfortable doing so. After a few weeks, he checked with me to know whether the job was done. I said it was not and told him I was not comfortable with his request. Although he was not in my reporting structure, he became angry and stormed off in a huff. Just a few days prior to my performance review, he assumed the role of my manager. Naturally, I was rated badly in that cycle. There was no real benefit of complaining to HR, as they don't take such issues seriously. So, all I could do was to grin and bear it. And that is what I did.'

Mr Singh was posted as a controller in a government accounting organization on 31 December. He was due for retirement on 31 March. He rushed to the new place of posting, which is in another city, and forced the incumbent who was under orders of transfer to hand over immediately, even though it was a public holiday. When asked why he was in such a hurry, he said, 'I can write the appraisals of my subordinates only if I supervise them for a minimum of three months. If I delay joining the new post, I will not be able to write the appraisal of the team. Unless that power is there, no one will respect me and they won't do what I want them to do.' Imagine the greed to have power even on the verge of retirement! Such bosses use the appraisal system as ammunition to get things done by hapless subordinates.

An officer of a large banking company had this to share: 'My boss, who is the general manager always delays the writing of annual appraisals beyond the deadline. He takes the maximum time to submit the appraisals to HR. When I refused to oblige him on a personal favour that I thought was very unethical, he even threatened me, stating that he was yet to write my appraisal!'

℞ Prescription for you, the boss

The efficiency, professional maturity, fairness and transparency that are hallmarks of an ideal leader will come through when he carries out an appraisal of his team members. One should take enough time to analyse the performance of each team member rather than doing it casually or in a hurry.

Precaution for you

Be honest when projecting your performance. At the same time, don't undermine your performance. You need not be elaborate on every possible failure or omission, but admit it if you feel that you require improvement in an area. Further, do not make comparisons with your colleagues. Acknowledge the specific contributions of a colleague, team or boss if you have achieved something exceptional with them. Do not forget to highlight, in sober tones, infrastructural inadequacy or any other impediments or challenges that came in the way of achieving your targets.

Precept for the organization

If performance standards and measures are not clearly communicated, the system cannot become efficient. The performance appraisal system should not only be a comprehensive tool linked to rewards, recognition and improvement of individuals, but should also be an effective instrument to redesign HR strategies and evaluate the adequacy of infrastructure and other resources. The organization should thus ensure that appraisals are written comprehensively, with fairness and objectivity. As far as possible, a system of 360-degree appraisal should be in place along with simple, speedy and effective resolution of grievances in this area.

The signs of recovery

In an organization where performance appraisals are comprehensive, fair, transparent, efficient and optimally linked to rewards and recognition, there will be fewer grievances, smoother interpersonal relationships, less attrition and more productivity.

Author in conversation with Wayne F. Cascio, PhD

Problem-solving approach in performance management

Do you think, even after the implementation of innovative performance management policies and tools, this is an area of perception of unfairness and consequent dissatisfaction in the employees worldwide?

There are solid payoffs for doing performance management well. If you work for an organization with a great performance management system, you will have a clear line of sight that links your work to the success of your organization—you will perform better in your work and you will probably be amply rewarded for the same. Studies show that organizations with such systems are 51 per cent more likely to outperform their competitors on financial measures, and 41 per cent more likely to outperform their competitors on non-financial measures (for example, customer satisfaction, employee retention, quality of products or services). Obviously, if performance management was easy to do, more firms would do it. One of the major reasons it is difficult to execute well throughout an entire organization is that performance management demands daily, not annual, attention from every manager. On top of that, managers at every level need to be held accountable for the development of the people who report to them. It is part of a continuous process of improvement over time.

Do you feel that there is still an authoritarian approach to appraisals, even though organizational structures and processes are otherwise becoming increasingly democratic?

I'm sure that many bosses still cling to the old 'tell-and-sell' approach to performance reviews, rather than adopting the more 'problem-solving' type of approach that has been demonstrated to be more effective. For example, in 2011, Google's Project Oxygen sought to identify what makes a good boss. To answer that question, researchers analysed performance reviews, feedback surveys and nominations for managerial awards. They found that the best bosses were even-tempered, made time for one-to-one meetings, helped employees solve problems by asking questions and took an interest in the lives and careers of their direct reports. Surprise: ranked eighth [on the list of qualities of good bosses] was the ability to perform technical work. Solid technical skills alone do not translate into a good boss. Google also found that better bosses translated into better bottom-line results.

What preparedness is expected from the employees while reporting performance to the boss and for performance counselling?

The reporting should be honest and comprehensive. One of the best things that employees (and managers) can do is to develop actual examples of behaviour (STARS—situation, task, action, and results) to support their judgements about the ratings they assign. Unfortunately, far too few of them actually do this. Despite all the problems associated with performance management, evidence indicates, at least in the US, that firms are not ready to abandon the system. In a recent survey, 94 per cent of firms said that they intend to continue using their performance-review systems.

Wayne F. Cascio, PhD is a distinguished professor in the University of Colorado and Robert H. Reynolds chair in Global Leadership. He is also the senior editor, *Journal of World Business*. Currently, he is occupying the position of academic chair, CU Executive MBA Program, The Business School, University of Colorado, Denver.

34

BOSSES AND THE BATHSHEBA SYNDROME

KING DAVID IS a character depicted in the Old Testament of the Bible. He was an ordinary shepherd who successfully confronted the nine-foot, bronze-armoured Philistine giant Goliath with a sling and a few stones. He became the king of Israel by defeating exploiters and enemies of the people of the nation. He was a very efficient administrator and was committed to delivering justice to his people. It is written that he was also a man of integrity. However, one single act of succumbing to his lust resulted in his downfall. While his men were at war, he spied a beautiful woman, Bathsheba, from his rooftop. Though he found that she was married to one of his army men, he forced her to be in a relationship with him. He sent her husband to the front lines of battle where he got killed. David then married Bathsheba and was severely rebuked by the Prophet Nathan who said, the 'sword will never depart from thine house'. David cried to God for the rest of his life in repentance: 'For I acknowledge my transgressions, and my sin is always before me. Against You, You only, have I sinned. And done this evil in Your sight.'

In an excellent analytical article in the *Journal of Business Ethics* way back in 1993, Ludwig and Longenecker[94] pointed out how successful people fail ethically at some point. According to them, a) success makes managers complacent and they can lose focus, b) it leads to privileged access to information, c) it gives them unrestrained control of organizational resources, and d) it inflates their belief in the personal ability to manipulate outcomes.

For example, many leaders at the pinnacle of success have been brought down because of charges of sexual misconduct. In most cases, allegations are aimed at making such persons give up their grip on the organization. Efficient and disciplined bosses have often had to leave organizations simply because of suspicion, even when such allegations are not proved.

There are many bosses who would like to have female companions. Some of them even invest in expensive houses to maintain absolute privacy when they are with such friends. The host of a popular late night show, had to apologize publicly after news of his affairs with female staff members came out. In an interview, he said, 'I hurt a lot of people. I have nobody to blame but myself. I am looking to find out why I behaved the way I behaved.'

Bhavya, a manager of a consumer durables manufacturing company said, 'I had to leave my first job due to sexual harassment—not by one guy, but by multiple bosses. Another lady and I were the first women sales employees in the company, employed by the management to deal with the activities of the union in the sales department. So the union guys decided to drive us off or make us conform by harassing us wherever we went. My immediate boss purposely gave me evening jobs so that he could accompany me and say uncomfortable things. But I couldn't speak up. I quit the job finally.'

According to the Equal Employment Opportunity Commission, discrimination based on gender, unwelcome advances or requests for sexual favours constitutes harassment in the United States. Similar laws exist in most countries. Many companies do not prohibit consensual sexual relationships within the company. Their business conduct policies say that if a consenting romantic or sexual relationship develops, it should be disclosed to the HR department.

Jacinta, who worked in a company at UAE, shared an incident: 'One of my colleagues, who is Lebanese, was reporting to our HR director; she was his executive secretary. Every day he would call her for closed-door meetings inside his cabin. Initially, the relationship was healthy; he would say that he was like a father to her. Over time however, he started commenting about her looks and dresses and passing vulgar comments. He also started sending her obscene texts. One day, during a meeting, she switched on the recording system in her mobile and recorded the conversation. With this, she escalated the matter to the CEO of the company. But the outcome was totally unexpected. She was the one dismissed from service. She went to the labour court and the police arrested the HR director. Finally, the matter was settled out of court and the HR director had to pay a huge compensation to the employee.'

The president and CEO of a multinational company that provided full-spectrum consulting, technology and business process outsourcing was shown the door after an investigation by a counsel engaged by the Board, where they found that he had a relationship with a subordinate employee; there was also an allegation of sexual

harassment. He had demonstrated outstanding leadership skills during his 10-year tenure. In a media release, the company admitted that he worked hard to establish the company as a leader in the IT industry. The gentleman had earlier headed the global operations of another IT giant till he was asked to quit on allegations of sexual harassment there as well. He was widely credited for his crucial contribution in making the company achieve very high turnover. The company had to pay the employee a whopping 3 million dollars in an out-of-court settlement.

There are several such incidents reported about successful leaders. The director general and CEO of an international agency with a 1.2 million membership had to resign on an allegation that he had sexually abused someone a few decades ago.

There are two factors common in the above cases: all the accused were in powerful positions and were successful leaders who had turned around their respective organizations. No organization would have liked to terminate them. Power and success can thus make people overconfident about their acceptance in the organization. With large teams and resources are at their disposal, they may begin to have a tendency to indulge in excesses. Further, people who depend on them become vulnerable to their actions. Also, in spite of their strong position as superiors, they may become weak before attractive women in the team.

℞ Prescription for you, the boss

Your power, access to resources and past achievements should propel you to be more disciplined and focused. Succumbing to momentary desires can dump you in a bottomless pit. Ensure that you do not get distracted by the wrong people or circumstances.

Precaution for you

A gentle reminder to your boss about the behavioural expectations from people in a senior position can sometimes be an effective response when faced with unbecoming advances. Be aware that simply because a person is your senior in terms of professional matters, he cannot exercise control over your personal life. By being vulnerable to such bosses, you demonstrate your weakness as well.

Precept for the organization

Organizations should ensure that leaders even at the highest levels are given inputs on how to sustain success and effectively regulate their conduct. There is also a need for proper gender-sensitivity training to take place, along with psychological and sociological assistance to employees to enable them to lead a positive work, family and social life.

The signs of recovery

Success and power do not intoxicate a person who is emotionally mature, ethically conscious, socially responsive and morally strong.

When the boss is a 'smart' communicator

a. 'Just listen to what I say. No questions please!' (Don't stick your stupid tongue out!)
b. 'I want the report within an hour. I don't care how you get it done.' (Get out of my room and start working on the report!)
c. 'I am busy. I believe in action, rather than your narration' (I don't have time to listen to your silly excuses!)
d. 'Who are you to suggest such things?' (You fool, you are nobody. Keep quiet!)
e. 'Who are you to decide this?' (You are just a worm. Who has delegated power to you?)
f. 'My boys are wonderful!' (I am very happy with these donkeys. They take a good load without cribbing)
g. 'I plan to nominate you for this training. Hope you are happy.' (I am a generous king who would like to shower surprise bounties to loyalists)
h. 'Peon, get coffee for us.' (I am going to give him a tough task)

i. 'If you are free, come to my chamber.' (I have some personal work to get done through you)
j. 'No comments' (How dare you ask that!)
k. 'I have also passed through your stages' (But I was not stupid like you!)
l. 'Congrats. You succeeded as you followed my directions so well' (You fool, don't take credit for the success. It is just because of my efforts to push things into your stupid head)

Read the next chapter to know who is a good communicator

35

BOSS SPEAKS IN LATIN; WE HEAR GREEK

COMMUNICATION IS THE key to success. There are many good leaders who became unpopular because of their failure to communicate appropriately. People often say, 'He is basically a nice man. But he doesn't know how to talk!'

A senior executive in a private sector bank told me, 'I do not know what the manager expects from me. He doesn't tell me whether he is happy or unhappy with my work. When I report, he just gives me a blank smile that I can't decipher.'

Eric Berne, renowned psychiatrist, the author of the book *Games People Play*[95] and the exponent of Transactional Analysis has researched the nature of communication between individuals. According to him, there are three ego states that are observable in every individual: Parent, Child and Adult. The parent is a 'taught concept', the child is a 'felt concept' and the adult is a 'learned concept'. When two people communicate, one person initiates a transaction (transactional stimulus) and the other person responds (transactional response). Simple Transactional Analysis involves identifying which ego state (parent, child or adult) in one person directed the stimulus and which ego state in the other person executed the response. Complementary transactions occur when the stimuli and response are as intended. But cross transactions occur when there is a mismatch between stimuli and response. This is because people perceive meanings not just by the words spoken but also the tone, emphasis on particular words, volume and other factors. This may lead to misinterpretation of what the other has said.

Albert Mehrabian[96] explained the relevance of non-verbal cues in communication. According to him, when an individual is speaking, 7 per cent of the listener's focus is on actual words, 38 per cent on the way the words are delivered, and 55 per cent on facial expressions.

As such, one can say that the relationship between the leader and his team is influenced by the nature of communication. The state of mind of the leader, especially when particular messages are communicated, is important in gauging responses from the team members along with the subsequent compliance or follow up.

A lady executive in a banking company shared this: 'When I asked my boss for a day's leave to look after my sick daughter, he asked me, "Don't you have your parents or in-laws or maids at home?" He didn't say whether the leave had been granted or not. He continued to look at my face with an expression that conveyed something like this: "Why didn't you think of a back-up plan before breeding?" I left his room quickly.'

Clarity and simplicity are the two essential attributes of good communication. Peter Loscher was the first top executive in the history of Siemens to be hired from outside the company. When he joined after leaving his post at Merck, he was apprehensive about the organizational culture and nature of communication in the new job. He narrates how he managed to drive change in Siemens in his article in the *Harvard Business Review*, November 2012. He found that Siemens employees were frustrated with the bureaucracy and wanted more independent decision-making. People felt that the corruption scandals were partly a failure of leadership. He said, 'If you want to change a big, complex organization like Siemens, you have to make your agenda known to people and you have to communicate in simple terms.'

There are many types of poor communicators among bosses. Here are a few types:

Judgemental	These bosses convey everything critically, giving an impression of lack of confidence in the capability of the other person. Such bosses are bad evaluators of work. They fail to appreciate others or couch their comments in a way that hinders the other person from understanding the real meaning.
Surreptitious	These bosses deliberately hide certain aspects in their communication. They want to hold the strings. They expect team members to be dependent on them for vital information.
Privileged	These bosses speak in a tone of superiority, giving the impression that the listener is lucky to get an audience with the boss. They are not interested in actually communicating the relevant material, and questions are not encouraged by them.
Gas-bag	These bosses speak unnecessarily without coming to the point. In the end, the listeners grope in the dark about the real agenda.
Pre-emptive	These bosses begin the conversation such that they put the other person on the defensive and prevent positive communication.
Utterly pessimistic	Their communication is depressing and rarely motivating.
Misleading	They give out contradictory facts and the real intent is unclear to others.

Written communication

Mittal is the head of a tax and accounting firm. He is very good at oral communication and meetings with him are always a pleasant experience. He has the habit of following up with the team through long mails on what was discussed and agreed upon in the meetings.

The problem the team faces is understanding what he has conveyed in writing. They get misled on the real intent of the mails, since he tends to add points not discussed earlier or ignore those that were discussed. Proper written communication is thus as important for the leader as oral communication. In oral communication, the communicator can instantly gauge the reactions of the other person and accordingly make amends through words or expressions. However, in written communication, there is a possibility that the recipient misunderstands and acts without waiting for clarification.

A good communicator knows what to communicate as well as how, when and where to do so.

Exercise 2

Are you a good communicator?
Test your Communication Quotient

(Mark your response below or in a separate sheet)

1. Whenever I communicate a matter to another person, I ensure that the other person gets it right by making it clear, or even by repeating it
   a. Always
   b. Many times
   c. Sometimes
   d. Never

2. When I am speaking to a group of about 10 people and two of them are talking to each other, then
   a. I tell them to stop talking to each other
   b. I ignore the cross-talk and continue speaking
   c. I wait for them to complete the conversation
   d. I wait for a little while and then request them politely to listen to me.

3. I tend to start speaking before the other person concludes his conversation
   a. Always
   b. Most of the time

    c. Sometimes
    d. Never
4. My family members tell me to lower my voice when I speak
    a. Many times
    b. Sometimes
    c. Rarely
    d. Never
5. My friends, colleagues or the audience have told me to speak a little louder
    a. Many times
    b. Sometimes
    c. Rarely
    d. Never
6. There are occasions when others have misunderstood what I have said, which has resulted in unpleasant responses
    a. Many times
    b. Sometimes
    c. Rarely
    d. Never
7. I have noticed a few people yawning when I am talking
    a. Many times
    b. Sometimes
    c. Rarely
    d. Never
8. I feel that others listen with a lot of interest whenever I narrate the story of a movie or an experience
    a. Many times
    b. Sometimes
    c. Rarely
    d. I don't share any such stories or experiences with others
9. After writing an email, I go through it before sending it
    a. Always
    b. Sometimes
    c. Rarely

d. I am too lazy for that
10. When someone asks me for directions to a place known to me, if I am hurrying for another task, I will
   a. Tell him I don't know the place, though I do know it
   b. Tell him the direction very fast, which I know that I have not conveyed clearly
   c. Tell him the direction quickly and as clearly as possible
   d. Patiently tell him the direction very elaborately, taking my time
11. When I am in the audience I would like to engage in conversation with the person near me when a speaker is addressing us
   a. I don't mind
   b. I do, sometimes
   c. I do, when the speaker is not noticing
   d. I rarely do that
12. Before I talk to a person (other than my family member or close friend) I think for a few seconds before each sentence about what to speak next
   a. Never
   b. Sometimes
   c. Most of the time
   d. Always
13. I feel that I am a good listener
   a. Yes, others have told me or I've heard them say that about me
   b. I like to listen to people more than talking to them
   c. I do not know
   d. Most of the time, it is me who is talking
14. I have faced occasions where, because of my use of certain words, others have abruptly or quickly ended the conversation with me
   a. Many times
   b. Sometimes
   c. Rarely
   d. Never

15. People say that I am a person of few words (or something like that)
    a. Many times
    b. Sometimes
    c. Rarely
    d. Never
16. People say that I am a chatterbox (or something like that)
    a. Many times
    b. Sometimes
    c. Rarely
    d. Never
17. I have been called on to give a speech
    a. Many times
    b. Sometimes
    c. Rarely
    d. Never
18. I have been asked to mediate to solve a problem, issue or misunderstanding between two people
    a. Never
    b. Rarely
    c. Sometimes
    d. Many times
19. People come seeking a suggestion, solution or remedy from me
    a. Never
    b. Rarely
    c. Sometimes
    d. Many times
20. During a conversation, people have told me to be cool and not get angry
    a. Never
    b. Rarely
    c. Sometimes
    d. Many times

Please refer to pages 256 to analyse your score

©Sibichen K. Mathew

Understand the boss's non-verbal communication

It's high time you got out of his room, if...
- He looks at the clock or his watch often
- He clasps his hands over his mouth and covers half of his nose
- His eyes go to the TV/computer/phone while you are chatting or sharing information
- He asks the attendant to take away the cups
- He starts moving to the edge of his seat
- He starts looking at the files on his desk
- He yawns
- He keeps looking elsewhere
- He looks at the visiting cards of the people waiting for him
- He signals the attendant to call the person waiting after you
- He closes his eyes for one full second or more
- He omits ordering tea/coffee, though he is used to doing so
- He sips his beverage faster than usual

36

THE PUPPET HAS A LONG TENURE

THERE WAS AN officer who complained that he was shifted more than 20 times to different posts within his organization in a span of two years. There was another who said that he was allowed to continue in a comfortable post for several years. Both these situations ruin a successful organization.

Mr Sharma joined as the manager in a large steel manufacturing company at the age of 22. He was elevated to higher positions because of his highly obedient nature. He always agreed with his bosses, even when he was sure that their ideas were not in the best interest of the company. For managers like Sharma, the major objective is not to 'rock the boat'. His eyes were set on the top post; all he wanted was a good grade from his boss. So for him, his boss was always right; he became adept at obeying the dictum of the boss.

A non-controversial figure is often preferred over one who is known to be forthright. People like Sharma are only too conscious of what they want and they willingly become puppets in the hands of their bosses. For them, the means justify the ends. We see many such puppets in the bureaucracy. They often also surround themselves with efficient but less ambitious officers. Mr Sharma and other similar people do not care about the organization, and only look out for their self-interest. Undoubtedly, under their stewardship, the organization suffers.

There are usually a few exceptions, however, who leave indelible impression in the organizations they work in. It took one T.N. Seshan[97] to show people the immense power of the Election Commission in India. In an earlier instance, General Manekshaw stood his ground when Prime Minister Gandhi demanded an early military intervention in East Pakistan in 1971.[98]

Advocates of stability or change?

Bosses can be broadly divided into two categories: those who are advocates of stability and those who champion changes. Bosses in each category have their unique leadership traits. Some such traits are given below:

Advocates of stability (Traits and position)	Champions of change (Traits and position)
Averse to new rules	Explore new processes
Feel time-tested strategies are best	Try new strategies
Believe organization is at its optimum performance	Feel that the organization has potential for further growth
Disinclined to take risks	Believe that risk-taking will lead to growth
Are agents of continuity	Are agents of change
Experimentation is unnecessary for them	Like to experiment
They do not take drastic decisions	Take quick decisions

Both stability and change are necessary in all organizations. Successful leaders can balance the two to explore new processes and strategies without completely letting go of time-tested traditions. But if they are controlled by their seniors, they might not be able to initiate change on their own at all.

A young and energetic officer commented about his boss: 'He neither acts nor reacts. He doesn't take risks or encourage risk-taking. He goes linear, never turning right or left.' Bosses who rule by the book, in spite of their understanding that many rules are redundant, stick to their archaic mindsets. They neither take steps to amend the rules nor deviate from them for the common good. They bring pseudo-stability to the organization without any effort.

The attributes of 'puppet' bosses in relation to responses to their bosses:

- They are sycophantic
- They indulge in flattery
- They are highly loyal
- They lack self-confidence
- They fear losing power
- They do not get out of their comfort zones
- They are undeterred by criticism from those who are under them
- They become incompetent over a period of time

In private organizations, such bosses are controlled by their bosses. But in public service organizations, the bosses are made puppets not only by the bosses inside but also by those outside. Bureaucrats in governments are often controlled by political masters in daily decision-making. In order to facilitate smooth control, politicians in power bring in their own people to hold important bureaucratic positions and let them stay as long as they want, often extending their tenure after their superannuation.

Dennis R. Young of Columbia State University, in his article[99] on puppet leadership, has stated that it is an instrumental kind of leadership with leaders behaving as agents rather than principals. 'Puppet leaders can be extremely damaging to the organization if their string-pullers have agendas in conflict with the organization's best interests and if they are appointed for their compliance rather than their competence.'

Puppet bosses create conventions that could make their successors helpless. Instead of leaving a legacy of courage, efficiency and innovation, they establish a structure that is weak and dependent on powers elsewhere.

℞ Prescription for you, the boss

Puppet bosses are disrespected by everyone in the organization. By blindly complying with bosses, even when you are not convinced of such decisions, you are putting your organization at risk. You are not fit to be called a leader if you do not have the skills to make your bosses understand what is good for the organization in the long run. It is better to look for another job rather than pledging yourself to inefficiency for the sake of personal comforts.

Further, do not make your team members your puppets by giving threats or promising rewards for toeing the line. Encourage creativity within your team and appreciate suggestions and constructive dissent.

Precaution for you

The indecisiveness and inefficiencies of a puppet boss should not deter you from doing what is right even if it displeases him. Most puppet bosses lack self-confidence and fear loss of power. Therefore, it is less likely that they will harm you personally for presenting a view contrary to what their boss wants you to do.

You need to be vigilant while executing the orders of a puppet boss by recording what transpired at each stage. You need to be smart enough to report adverse results as early as possible.

Precept for the organization

Organizations should ensure that sufficient autonomy is given to leaders at each level of hierarchy. There should be relative stability of tenure at each position with ample scope for elevation if one's performance is rated well in accordance with a transparent assessment using acceptable benchmarks that are communicated in advance.

The signs of recovery

Creativity and efficiency are direct results of independence. Leaders and team members in such an environment gain mutual respect and recognition.

37

BOSSES AND THE IMAGE-MAKERS

WE HAVE HEARD of 'window dressing' of balance sheets by corporates. There are many bosses who window dress themselves too. They desire constant adulation from people around them. While some of the major corporate heads appoint brand ambassadors from either within the organization or outside, other bosses cultivate fans to sing paeans to them.

Michael Shea, who was a press secretary to the Queen of England and also a member of the diplomatic corps, had the opportunity to interact closely with many heads of states and international leaders. He wrote, 'The real qualities of a leader are often in inverse proportion to the number of image-makers on his or her staff.'[100] He further stated, 'Strong leaders speak for themselves. Weak leaders and weak organizations need to be dressed up in the clothes of authority and wisdom by the image-makers of life.'

Image-boosting through the media

Image-makers take the help of the media to show organizational success as being the result of their unique efforts. Vaara and Monin in their study[101] have found that leaders and their actors use the mass media as an 'arena of discursive strategizing' to justify the actions of the leadership.

Chen and Meindl[102] have studied the construction of leadership images in the popular press. According to them, the media has a tendency to interpret organizational outcomes by reference to leaders. Sinha, Inkson, and Barker used dramaturgical perspective to analyse Air New Zealand's failed acquisition of Ansett Australia to conclude how the CEO, media, intermediaries and various other stakeholders 'co-created an unfolding drama marked by the CEO escalating the firm's commitment to the failing acquisition as a way of maintaining an illusion of control, which helped preserve the CEO's celebrity identity'.[103] Most of the image-driven actions do not lead to enduring success.

Various methods

Image-centric bosses employ many methods to maintain and uplift their image through their image-makers. Some of them are given below:

a. Get media publicity by projecting the achievements of the organization and creating an impression that his strategies have resulted in the success.
b. Get ghostwriters to write books or prepare articles for them to publish in the mainstream media.
c. Get their speeches written by professional writers and orators.
d. Get content writers to push write-ups on their achievements in websites, blogs, online encyclopaedias, social networking sites, and so on.
e. Get invited to speak in public programmes where there is media publicity.
f. Get their organizations to sponsor major social, cultural and educational activities and gain opportunity to be in the limelight.
g. Get themselves featured in advertisements, brochures, marketing videos, and other publicity material more often than required.

Digital narcissism

Many leaders have an active presence in online groups and platforms. There are dozens of networking platforms with a dialogic structure to exchange views on anything across the world instantly. People compete to have more followers than others and popular posts and comments. In order to have a vibrant presence, some bosses even outsource the content dissemination to experts.

A celebrity-turned-entrepreneur said, 'I was so busy in my earlier role as an artist and I never had any time focusing on creating a popular profile in the digital social networking platforms. I knew that there were several pages created by others about me. But I later found that the contents and comments in those pages were actually not in good taste and sometimes totally disgusting. Now, I've started my own official page but am looking for someone to update it on my behalf.'

Appointing image consultants

Many corporate bosses have benefited from the recent flourishing profession of image consulting. Bosses hire the services of an image consultant to get guidance on improving their physical appearance (grooming, dressing, body makeover and so on), behavioural patterns and communication. It is interesting to note that consultancies are available now not just for bosses but also for team members.

One-way image-building is safe; but there are risks in the two-way process!

Conventional image-building strategies through print and visual media are difficult but not risky. However, the image-building through online media platforms is easy but tends to invite quick responses from the public. This is a tightrope many choose to walk; they may even become adept at avoiding the quicksand. Anyone can make a comment or share content that damages the leader's image. Other leaders wear their heart on their sleeve and pay the price. There are some leaders who quit the social media platform after getting unpleasant responses.

℞ Prescription for you, the boss

The aura of superiority or infallibility projected by you or by your image-makers can have a short life. Only the image people carry about you based on what you really are and what you really do can make you stand in good stead. In the end, actions speak louder than words!

Precaution for you

You are safe. You need not worry much about the boss's frantic efforts to boost his image.

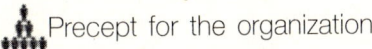Precept for the organization

In the short run, definitely, the organization will gain a lot out of the image makeover of its bosses. As such, resources for this should be invested by the organization rather than the bosses themselves; it would make the act more sensible and professional. However, organizations need to be mindful of the fact that images that are bought are in no way a match for images that are gained through excellence and authenticity.

The signs of recovery

Successful organizations and exemplary leaders will have a large number of people sharing a good word about them without any prompting.

38

WHICH ANIMAL ARE YOU AND YOUR BOSS?

ALL HUMAN BEINGS pass through the cycle of birth, growth, maturity, decline and death. Most organizations, too, move along a cycle similar to biological organisms, with birth, growth, maturity and a decline or revitalization stage.[104] Does leadership also have a lifecycle? How long can one be effective in a particular leadership role? If organizations decline but have scope for revitalization, can leaders also enter a stage of revitalization after their decline?

This has nothing to do with the age of the leader. It is about the number of years one has been doing a specific leadership task. Will that person remain the same, or on a progressive or declining phase? Will his technical competence, organizational efficiency, intellectual

acumen, reputation and social skills remain unscathed through the years?

It is interesting to compare the life of a person who has spent long years in a large organizational setting with life in the animal kingdom. One could give leaders at various stages of the leadership lifecycle certain attributes, just like the Chinese Zodiac has. Based on the observation of the attitudes and behavioural patterns of some officers, the following leadership lifecycle traits can be delineated.

Leader	Animal	Traits
1 to 4 years of entry	Tiger	Calm but rebellious Patient but short-tempered Fearsome but affectionate Energetic and enthusiastic
5 to 10 years	Lion	Confident and critical Arrogant Occasional bouts of laziness Craves for more power Wants to be the leader Radical creativity (in spite of an absolute absence of creativity in the organization, the individual can be creative)
11 to 20 years	Horse	Starts enjoying the power Picks up speed. Is proactive.
21 to 30 years	Elephant	Incremental creativity (if the organization and the environment is creative, the individual also becomes creative. Otherwise not!)
Above 30 years	Cat	Generally mild. Mostly lazy and sleepy. Rarely grumbles.
Just before retirement	A mix of Lion and Horse	Tries to regain the old power and glory. Moves fast because time is limited!

The above changes can be the reason why people leave the organization if there is better opportunity elsewhere. This happens mostly in the private sector, where there are enough avenues to be out as a lion and then regain entry as a tiger in another organization rather than transitioning to the stage of elephant or cat in the earlier one. However, in government and public sectors, most leaders tend to pass through the inevitable stages for comfort and security and also because of lack of external opportunities.

When a person occupies the same position for a fairly long time, it is expected that he will perform with efficiency as he is well experienced. Unfortunately, in many organizations one sees the reverse happening. It is perceived that the boss's efficiency drops after reaching its peak during long occupancy of a post. These bosses neither understand nor admit that their efficiency has taken a toll. It is not that they have become lethargic or bored with their work; from their point of view, they put more effort in the supervisory role and look much more deeply into the work of their team. Such strategies, ideas and approaches would not find favour with a young team with a different perspective. Bosses may also not appreciate the need to change strategies due to changes in circumstances. If they are not receptive to proposals for changes desired by the team, there will be dissatisfaction. A prolonged tenure thus causes obsolescence.

Chief Learning Officer (CEB), a member-based advisory firm, found in a study[105] that organizations with well-executed leadership transition processes can boost revenue by as much as 5 per cent. In another study by Xueming Luo, Vamsi K. Kanuri and Michelle Andrews,[106] it was found that the CEO's tenure affects performance. Though they say that the longer a CEO serves, the more the firm–employee dynamic improves, the study clearly found that a long tenure results in them becoming attached to the status quo, making them less responsive to vacillating customer preferences.

Leadership transition is a tough decision

Changing a person who is occupying a high position and who has transformed into an elephant or a cat can be a very tough decision for the management. The longer the person stays in the post, the more difficult is the task of changing him. Getting a fresh incumbent may be easy; the difficulty is more in finding a suitable alternative position for the person to be replaced. Often, the management has to do so to satisfy his ego and make the leadership transition smoother. When a transition is required at higher levels, the decision in this regard is taken by a few individuals who are above that particular position. For example, if the company wants to change the joint managing director, the decision to inform the present incumbent, promise him a suitable alternate position or compensation and find a better replacement is on the chairman and chief managing director or equivalent officer.

Embarrassment, if any, is experienced in the context of the leadership transition process by the senior management or the officer to be replaced, but can be avoided if there is a well-established policy in this regard. There can be fixed tenure for all senior and important posts, with extensions given only in exceptional cases. This can reduce unnecessary expectations on the part of the incumbent. The scope for an extension of tenure for exceptional performance can also be a motivation for him to put in his best effort.

No one will value your long experience or seniority if you can't provide the right leadership and handle tasks enthusiastically. You would be prudent to assess your capability in your leadership role and gauge your acceptability within the team. Be courageous to ask for a change if your bosses indicate that most of your team members are not comfortable with your style of functioning.

Precaution for you

Be patient, understanding and appreciative of your 'saturated' boss, who could either be a victim of a faulty promotion policy or his own 'learned helplessness'. Sharing your point of view politely and smoothly could help in resolving issues to a great extent.

Precept for the organization

Organizations should have a strong leadership transition policy to replace those at the top if they're found to be unproductive or counterproductive.

The signs of recovery

Organizations, whether old or young, will continue to be at their best if leaders at all levels are creative, enthusiastic, aware and proactive.

39

THE INSCRUTABLE BOSS!
YOU ARE BEING WATCHED

THIS IS A snooping world. Every action is being watched by people around. The way you walk, talk, act, react, eat and drink can be noticed, tracked and shared by others. There are many who are keen to gather details about you, your interests, your relationships and so on. They get data from whatever sources are available: friends, office staff, driver, maids and anyone else with whom you have frequent interaction.

When you are elevated to a higher position you are inviting a certain amount of risk. To an extent, you can lose your freedom of going unnoticed. There are many leaders who strive hard all along to catch the attention of people. Once they emerge as important persons, they strive to hide themselves from the crowd. What an irony!

This is an era of constant electronic surveillance everywhere on everyone. It could be by the state, private enterprises or individuals. In an increasingly insecure and unsecure world, there is a strong dependence on gadgets and technologies that can track properties, people and their behaviour. Even the media looks for personal secrets of important people. Much of the mainstream media sells gossip that mostly centre on the private acts of people partially based on information gathered clandestinely. Sting and under-cover operations are conducted in the most unethical manner in many cases. Gadgets for snooping are easily available and affordable. There are several wearable devices that can secretly record people or events as well.

As such, even casual conversations and opinions of high-ranking officials, senior corporate bosses or powerful leaders can be obtained through informal chats and transmitted to other organizations for 'necessary' analysis or conclusions. What is shocking is that this kind of 'secret' data is often leaked to the public.

The inscrutable bosses

There are some bosses who make sure they don't get captured in a weak moment. They keep their thoughts, perceptions and plans absolutely secret even from their closest colleagues such that no one can predict their next steps. This habit, while helpful to an extent, especially when the leader holds sensitive positions can cause issues if the person likes to be inscrutable for no logical or significant reason. Then it might simply be a personality trait.

If a person gives an impression of masking their real intentions, that can be seen as plain dishonesty. Robert Greene in his book *48 Laws of Power* had this[107] to say: a) 'use smoke screens (a poker face) to disguise your actions', b) 'use decoyed objects of desire and red herrings to throw people off scent', and c) 'false sincerity is one powerful tool that will send your rivals on a wild goose chase'. He called this 'wisdom'. However, such behaviour is nothing but deception. A true leader can't deceive people permanently. The famous quotation attributed to Jacques Abbadie (in French) and Abraham Lincoln is apt in this context: 'You can fool all the people part of the time, or you can fool some people all the time, but you cannot fool all the people all the time.'

Inscrutability is neither a virtue nor a good leadership strategy. It is a ploy used by those who need to hide their incapability as leaders. The more inscrutable you are, the more you might be tracked by inquisitive people. Unpredictable and secretive leaders also create an environment of mistrust in the organization.

A leader shows the way

A leader need not worry about what others perceive in or about him if he has nothing to hide. If the boss showcases contradictory behaviour or responses in public and private, then he should be worried about his impression on people. Stever Robbins wrote, 'Once you know the behaviours you want to create in your organization, start exhibiting yourself.'[108] In every team, members look at their leader closely to understand his behavioural pattern and responses. The conduct of the leader influences the team members. Therefore, leaders need to display exemplary behaviour within the organization and in the public domain.

Dishonour Roll

You must have heard of payrolls in corporates. But have you heard of **Dishonour Rolls secretly circulated within companies?**

It is said that in many corporates a list of 'dangerous' top executives is circulated among freshers. It would take a lot of time for someone to understand the nature and real intention of bosses if they are too inscrutable. Information is secretly shared about such bosses within the team. In one organization, a few lady executives update and pass around the list of males who have a 'weakness' for women and those who very 'authoritatively' pursue the art of womanizing. They categorize the list based on the nature and type of person, strategies, extent of harm and so on. They put apt labels for each category like 'lech', 'mouth looker', 'creepy', 'touchy' and so on. The message is loud and clear: 'Try to escape from them. If attacked, don't complain. You will be thrown out.' This dishonour roll is only about the powerful senior bosses and is made accessible to closed groups on social networking sites.

℞ Prescription for you, the boss

Imagine that you are sitting in a chamber with glass walls all around. Your professional life—and also your personal life to a great extent—is of interest to those around you. They will watch you whether you like it or not. Do you want to be laughed at and ridiculed while you sit in your chamber? If not, then be at your best when you are the boss.

Precaution for you

Watch your boss if you can't avoid it. But don't emulate what you see as not exemplary. Also, understand that information gathered through snooping would not add value to your job or personality.

Precept for the organization

The organization should take care to prevent undue invasion of privacy of any individual by itself or by others.

The signs of recovery

Transparency in one's responses brings trust and loyalty. If the boss is open and consistent in his actions, that would reverberate everywhere in the organization.

40

HOW CREATIVE ARE YOU AND YOUR BOSS?

WHAT IS THE most entertaining and relaxing time for you in the day? Is it during recreational activities like watching television, browsing the internet, playing games, partying with friends, chatting with a pal, enjoying a meal, listening to your favourite music or watching a play or a match? Most of us agree that one or more of the above can give us immense enjoyment and satisfaction. They are indeed very relaxing. To sum up, recreation is easy! Then what is difficult?

Creation is what is difficult and challenging. It is only creation that can trigger growth. Recreation means maintaining the status quo; enjoying and re-enjoying what already exists. Creation brings in change to make something new or better. Many of those who lead organizations prefer to trudge along the beaten path rather than blaze a trail. Indeed, they may have the knowledge and the expertise but are apathetic about change.

Psychologists and neuroscientists say that most people use only about 1 per cent of their brain's capabilities. We are averse to using our brain even to recollect certain things we have learnt. Why are we so reluctant to use our intellect for creativity? Does this have to do with our reluctance to come out of our comfort zones? Or is it because often the top management is risk-averse? According to Edward De Bono,[109] the need to be right all the time is the biggest obstacle to new ideas. Does the fear of failure then hold us back? To quote De Bono again, 'Creativity involves breaking out of the established patterns in order to look at things in a different way.' Creativity makes organizations withstand the march of time. Yet, how many organizations or leaders proactively promote creativity?

Jack Zenger and Joseph Folkman analysed[110] the behaviour of 30,000 managers, as seen through the eyes of 300,000 of their peers, direct reports and bosses on 360-degree evaluations. They found that the 'sins of the bad boss are far more often those of omission, not commission'. Some of the fatal flaws contributing to the failure of a boss are a) resistance to new ideas, b) failure to develop others, and c) lack of vision.

We often hear people saying, he is born creative! This is to show that creativity can be in one's genes; however that does not mean it cannot be acquired. The 'six thinking hats' method by Edward de Bono is an excellent process through which any creative idea can be processed, developed, tested and implemented. In this method the group deliberates on a) analysing data and information (white hat), b) allowing people to express their emotions and fears (red hat), c) critical analysis of pros and cons (black hat), d) exploring solutions and feasibility (yellow hat), e) soliciting further creative ideas and alternatives (green hat) and f) organizing and controlling varied ideas and initiatives (blue hat).

Great place to Work® in collaboration with *Fortune* Magazine identified 100 of the best companies to work with in the United States in 2013. SAS occupied the second place in the list. The employee-focused philosophy of SAS is: 'If you treat employees as if they make a difference, they will make a difference.' SAS CEO Jim Goodnight wrote[111] about the company's culture: 'A culture that rewards innovation, encourages employees to try new things and yet doesn't penalize them for taking chances, and a culture that cares about employees' personal and professional growth.' Unless an environment is created for the team to be creative without fear of criticism for failure, people will not take up challenges that lead to innovation. Teresa M. Amabile, former dean of Harvard Business School wrote: 'when creativity is killed, an organization loses a potential weapon: new ideas. It can also lose the energy and commitment of its people.'[112]

Bosses who are cognitive misers

We have heard of people who are very miserly when it comes to spending their money. But there are leaders in many organizations who prefer to give their brains a rest once they are elevated as bosses. They think it is the job of the junior officials and executives to find solutions.

These bosses are cognitive misers, and spend most of their time travelling or relaxing. They expect their team to give the final analysis and solutions for any problem so that they can decide on the best option without any effort.

A true leader is one who is continuously in learning mode. His collapse starts the day he stops learning. Many leaders, though very senior or old, maintain their acceptability among people through their ability to learn and knack for spotting opportunities. They refuse to fade away and they are often at the forefront of the battle to change and innovate.

The retirement mode

Why do some very senior bosses stop strategizing or contributing creatively? Do they feel obsolete as they see technologies changing, perspectives getting altered and new goals being set by the new generation? Do they think that they should, in fact, give a rest to their intellect at the end of their career rather than slog as earlier? A feeling of depression can certainly set in among many bosses as the time of their retirement approaches. Some would also feel that they have lost the intellectual capacity to exert an influence on younger members. A few may fear that their advice and views will no longer be accepted.

G. Bennis and J. Thomas quoted[113] 75-year-old Mel Brooks, who won 12 Tonys (theatrical awards) as saying, 'I don't look in the mirror and I don't look at the calendar'. In a quote attributed to

Mark Twain, it is said that aging is in the mind and if one doesn't mind, it doesn't matter.

A lethargic boss can kill the creativity of the team. Any attempt at creativity invariably includes elements of risk and out-of-the-box thinking. However, the courage and preparedness to unlearn is a necessary prerequisite for creativity too. The biggest block in the road to creativity is the fixation with what one has already learnt and put into practice. How can we break these shackles?

Recipes for creativity for you, the boss

1. Trust the team
2. Encourage their creative ideas
3. Don't brand those who give creative suggestions as rebels
4. Provide appropriate resources for developing ideas
5. Facilitate brainstorming within and among teams
6. Remember that creative ideas can come from anyone at any level
7. Be available—creativity germinates in an environment of proximity and openness
8. Organize workshops and creative exercises for team members
9. Evaluate and decide on creative proposals as quickly as possible
10. Experiment with ideas
11. Conduct periodical creativity audits or opportunity audits

Recipes for creativity for you

1. Nurture any idea that emerges
2. Be quick to judge the risks
3. Be prepared to face failure
4. Share ideas with a few trusted people
5. Be convinced about your ideas and be courageous to take the plunge
6. No purpose is served by hiding your idea, fearing replication by others

7. Take the help of a support group
8. Do critical evaluation of the utility of your idea
9. Don't always think that the solution at hand is the best one
10. Expect the unexpected. Your efforts might bring something better than what you have already
11. Be prepared to unlearn to learn something new

41

BOSS LEAVES; BOMB EXPLODES

HERE IS AN organization. Everyone below works not for the organization, but for the boss. The boss thinks he is the only one who thinks and all others are still (and always will be) either *Ramapithecus* or *Proconsul*.[114] Therefore, he expects them to work like machines for him. As his children are settled abroad, the boss, who stays with his wife, has plenty of time on hand. He has suddenly become overzealous, and has started sermonizing that work is worship. When the boss is around, the office atmosphere is stressful. People are nervous; they shout at jokes and cry at shouts. They compete to please the one and only boss. Top managers are satisfied if the ferocious boss says one word in a normal tone or condescends to give one gentle look, since they are so rare. Most of the times, middle-level managers get 'sound' pieces of advice from the boss that reverberate everywhere and kill the peace. In this organization, no employee, irrespective of their key designation, has clarity on the strategies to be followed. They do not dare to air their opinions, views or suggestions to the boss or to colleagues and subordinates. Everyone acts and reacts in accordance with the screenplay and direction of the autocratic boss. They are not expected to deviate even a little from the direction given by the boss.

The bomb explodes

For every boss, however mighty he feels, there will come a day when he is out. Then the real bomb explodes. The office becomes chaotic. Employees become directionless. Systems collapse. No one knows what the next steps are. The organization goes through a rough patch at this stage!

Employees at all levels may feel relieved and enjoy the departure of the boss who made their life hell. They might even share their traumatic experiences with all and sundry, venting their feelings without fear. Some might take long leave to get rejuvenated. Others might start concentrating on their long pending family commitments. They realize that during those hectic periods under the demanding boss, their children have grown up. The organization as a whole goes into static mode. Employees might then begin to feel the absence of a driving force. They have already lost their creativity and look to the next boss to give them a push.

Steep downfall

Autocratic, egotistic and pretentious bosses like the one depicted above kill an organization's overall vitality and creativity. Power, if bestowed upon one individual exclusively and disproportionately, is detrimental to the organization in the long run. Employees here would not have any loyalty, morale, mutual understanding, social embeddedness, creativity or job satisfaction. They lose self-confidence and initiative. The organization would show quantitative outputs that are not enduring. It would scale to new heights, but a steep downfall would also be imminent after the exit of the old boss. Bright employees would look for better opportunities elsewhere to demonstrate their creativity, while the lazy, risk-averse and average performers would not stir out of the comfort zone that routine work provides. External stakeholders would react sharply to the inefficiency in the organization at some point, and would question the rationale of its existence. All because of one boss who failed to create an efficient, motivated, confident and creative team!

The need for psychological empowerment

An organization consists of people with varied personality traits, attitudes and behavioural patterns. Many organizations that have built provisions and machinery to give opportunities for strategic planning and high-level responsibilities fail in appropriately tailoring them according to the interests, capabilities and potential of individuals. Various scholars have identified[115] the benefits of psychological empowerment such as a) stronger commitment to tasks at hand, b) greater initiative to perform, c) greater perseverance when faced with obstacles, d) preparedness to learn, e) optimism, and f) better job satisfaction. Most organizations, therefore, fail to lay out rules, procedures, and conventions that facilitate psychological empowerment. It is necessary that the organization or the apex leadership conduct suitable analysis, evaluation and training among team members to understand and identify their true potential before involving them in strategic planning.

℞ Prescription for you, the boss

Realize that you are not indispensable and are not going to be able to take the organization with you to your grave. Nurture leaders within the organization.

 Precaution for you

Don't allow your creativity and enthusiasm to get sapped. Try to make your boss see your intelligence or efforts by suggesting exceptional strategies and solutions that even he would have not thought of. He might not appreciate you, but it might unscrew his uptightness a little.

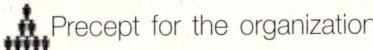 Precept for the organization

An organization should have a mission and vision formulated through collective thinking of all who matter, and not just based on the ideas, aspirations and expectations of a single individual.

There should be a well-designed set of dynamic operating procedures for decision-making and implementation that are not influenced by only one person who leads the organization. Plus, senior managers should have clear roles and powers to courageously take on the boss if they find that the latter is imposing decisions solely from his point of view.

Most importantly, the boss needs to be advised and his decisions need to be evaluated by a group of independent experts. Some super bosses have the knack of controlling these advisory boards as well. In such cases, the authority for or under whom the boss works needs to take the call.

The signs of recovery

Efficient organizations have the habit of creating leaders after leaders, such that the new ones pick up the baton effortlessly.

> An ideal boss would nurture the person next in line to enable him to shoulder important responsibilities at short notice. The well-known Telugu movie released in 1997, *Shankarabharanam*, portrayed an Indian classical musician named Shankara Shastri and his life devoted to music. During his last public performance, when he was unable to continue a raga because of chest pain, one of his disciples who wished to continue his legacy quickly picked up where he had left off and continued the song. In much the same vein, every organization needs to have a successor ready to fill the void of the boss with equal efficiency and finesse so that the organization moves forward without missing a beat.

Author in conversation with Kiran Mazumdar-Shaw

'Empowering the team: The key to success'

How can leaders make team members feel important?
- I truly believe that empowering people with decision-making builds a good work ethic. My leadership style has been about motivating people through self-belief and self-assertion. I believe in performance through job ownership and accountability. I believe that people need to 'own job responsibility' rather than merely 'perform tasks'.

Many bosses do not tolerate criticism. What is your view?
- I particularly respect people who share their responsibility rather than closely guard their knowledge and thereby lead by command. I respect fairness even in criticism. I like people who are frank, honest and upfront. The type of people I least respect are those that are indecisive and hide behind excuses. Lack of decisions is the root cause of our present economic decline and wasted resources.

What is true empowerment in an organization?
- I believe in delegating decision-making and inculcating pride in a job well executed. Most of all, acknowledging a team's contribution to success. All this would lead to empowerment.

How does attrition at very senior levels affect the organizations?
- This is a worrying trend that stems from aimless opportunism. If it is just to make a little more money, it is foolish as it erodes experience. If it is an experimental step to assess the optimal job, then a few job hops are fine, but it must stop at some stage to allow you to build capability. Attrition does cost organizations very dearly. It is important for HR to build a value proposition that leads to enduring employment through a good career path

Ms Shaw heads India's leading biopharmaceuticals enterprise, Biocon. She has been named among *TIME* magazine's 100 most influential people in the world. Ms Shaw is also the chairman, Board of Governors, Indian Institute of Management, Bangalore (Bengaluru). Her most cherished awards are the national awards, Padma Shri (1989) and Padma Bhushan (2005) presented to her by the President of India, for her pioneering efforts in industrial biotechnology. She heads a team of about 7,500 well-qualified employees.

42

THE MESSIAH RETURNS

N.R. NARAYANA MURTHY took retirement from Infosys in 2011. He was instrumental in building the company and spent an average of 16 hours a day and 330 days in a year away from home. When he took retirement in 2011, he said, 'The best analogy that I can think for the separation between Infosys and me is that of one's daughter getting married and leaving her parents' home.'

When Infosys was listed on the NASDAQ, sitting on a high stool at the headquarters of the stock exchange in New York, Murthy borrowed the words of Neil Armstrong to tell the world

how important it was for an Indian company to be listed on the NASDAQ. Infosys is one of the few companies that have given about Rs 50,000 crore (at stock prices at the end of 2011) of stock options to its employees. Every employee who joins Infosys is a stockholder. While leaving Infosys, he said in an interview, 'I definitely think I can live in peace, as I am definitely sure that these (new leaders) are very capable people. They are, of course, very kind to say good things about me. But I think they are in many ways smarter than me.'[116]

Unfortunately, Narayana Murthy was wrong in his judgement. Infosys did not have a rosy path once he left. The new leaders tried all kinds of strategies. At some point, it was understood that there was no option but to bring Murthy back. He returned to his post to manage operations directly.

Narayana Murthy is not a lone Messiah in corporate resurrections. There have been many such powerful miracle-makers who were asked to return or help to calm storms after they left the companies to their successors or mentees.

Michael Dell founded the eponymous company Dell in 1984 and was its chairman and CEO for more than 20 years. He quit his position as CEO in 2004, but had to return to resolve serious strategic issues.

Steve Jobs was considered a rigid zealot while he was in Apple during his first stint, and not many were unhappy when he left. Faced with nose-diving performance and stiff competition, however, the Board brought him back to be at the helm of affairs.

Starbucks chairman, Howard Schultz, also had to return as CEO to save the company, whose stocks plummeted by 50 per cent in one year, from drowning in the rough sea of competition.

Organizations are created with a mission and vision established by their founders. The cultural history and personality of the founders greatly influence the culture of the organization. It is the founding members who recruit the first team for execution of their plans. Edgar H. Schein[117] wrote that founders usually have a major impact on how the group initially defines and solves its external adaptation and internal integration problems. He said, 'Founders not only have a high level of self-confidence and determination, but they typically have strong assumptions about the nature of the world, the role that organizations play in the world, human nature and relationships, how truth is arrived at, and how to manage time and space.' This may be why many successors fail to assimilate the unique vision, skills and confidence of the founders or strong predecessors. It is also possible that the leaders of an organization lose touch with the vision and drift away to goals and strategies contrary to the original objectives. This is not noticed as long as the results are good. However, when the leaders fail to deliver what they are expected to, there might be a crisis of leadership. At that point, people within and outside the organization look for a Messiah to bail them out.

What are the characteristics of 'Messiah' bosses?

- Charismatic, but very firm
- Sometimes labelled as narcissist as they are tough, preferring their own ideas to those of others
- Either they have formulated the mission and vision themselves or are thorough with the same
- Clear about strategies and very good at communicating them
- Emotionally attached to organizational values
- Have uncompromising attitude towards organizational goals
- Intolerant of anyone who deviates from the organizational ethos

Is a strong Messiah a liability?

It is generally thought that founding fathers or leading influential mentors of any organization cannot or will not change their cultural ethos and personality in tune with the rapidly changing world. From what we have discussed above, our answer would be an emphatic 'No'. They are so only because they can rescue the organization from challenges and dangers. This means that they have had a cultural ethos and personality that can survive and tackle issues irrespective of the nature and gravity of the problem. Also, they are willing to embrace changes that are necessary for the organization to grow and expand. Thus, these bosses are different from authoritarian bosses who tend to force their ideas and strategies on the organization without being open to suggestions from below or outside. Messianic bosses are willing to nurture young talent and receptive to innovations suggested by anyone. The availability of a strong 'Messiah' is thus an asset for the organization.

Overdependence on the Messiah

How long should the organization depend on the Messiah for its survival? The maximum period, undoubtedly, is his lifetime. Overall, overdependence on the leader can be detrimental to the organization. How could the senior-most leaders, with vast experience in large companies like Infosys, Dell, Apple and Starbucks, struggle when their mentors bid goodbye?

Overdependence can happen mainly in two circumstances: First, when the senior-most leader (who is to reappear as a Messiah in the future) involves himself more than required and controls the company without giving independence to the people below him. Instead of leaving the crucial decisions to the layer below, he holds sway till the very last minute. The moment the leader walks away, there is a huge vacuum. Second, the power and authority are disproportionately skewed in favour of the leader till his exit, with only a minor share available with the second layer. Added to this, the power and discretion conferred on the leaders of the second layer are the same or just marginally higher as compared to his team members. This creates difficulty for the team members to accept the new leader as someone whom they need to trust, depend on and support just like their earlier leader. It is quite fashionable to argue that we need leaders and not one leader on the top. The point here is that no organization can survive without a strong leader who can perform the role of a neutral unifier.

It is thus the duty of the top leadership to nurture a strong team and groom a second line of leadership to pick up the mantle of leading the company. Otherwise, when they look back they will see their empire crumbling and struggling due to a leadership crisis and strategic confusion. No genuine mentor would like such a state of affairs.

 Prescription for you, the boss

You should be aware that you need to leave the ropes to the next layer of leaders sooner or later. It is your duty to nurture confidence in the leaders below you to take independent decisions. You need to give them enough opportunity to take and execute challenging decisions and responsibilities, so don't insist on your 'stamp' on them!

 Precaution for you

You can't stay in a comfort zone, looking at your boss for help at every step. Your overdependence on your boss can result in your team losing confidence in you.

Precept for the organization

If feasible, there should be a fixed tenure or retirement age for the people on top. In post-retirement mentoring, leaders should not be overinvolved in the day-to-day affairs of the organization. Clear powers and responsibilities with appropriate independence should be given to the senior layers of leadership.

The signs of recovery

A new leader takes the organization to further heights inspired by the mentoring, independence and lessons learned from his own crucial decisions of the past, and the challenges he faced before taking over from his senior. He need not run to a Messiah every now and then.

43

THE BOSSES AND THE EXPATS

SONIA MIRCHANDANI IS of Indian origin, but was born and brought up in a foreign country. Her ancestors migrated to that country a century earlier from India. She does not know Indian languages. She spoke the native language of the country with an accent just like any other person of that country did. Sonia earned outstanding grades in the universities and worked in various companies in senior posts. She is more than 45 years old now. She wished in vain: 'Can I ever get rid of my colour to avoid the cryptic remarks and branding?' She shared this: 'First time when a girl in my third grade called me a "Paki" while we had a tussle in the game field I didn't understand what it was. Later I heard that word when I got up to give my seat in the bus to an elderly lady, who refused to occupy my seat. I cried uncontrollably that night when I understood that even after a century my family was considered an outcast. Even at work, I was repeatedly discriminated against by a native boss there.'

If Sonia felt that she was being treated differently even after her family had been in that country for more than a hundred years, what would be the plight of people who temporarily migrate to another country for work? If the employers and members cannot offer equal treatment to expats, it can create serious psychological, social, and economic problems for migrants.

For many decades, countries have been dependent on skilled manpower from other countries to fill in the local supply gap. People leave their native land and culture to earn a living and also to improve their economic standards. Benyamin's book

Goat Days[118] depicted a real story of a young man from southern India who pursued his dream to get a job in a Gulf country, and ended up as a shepherd in a sterile wasteland. When a friend mentioned that there was a visa for sale to go to a Gulf country, Najeeb didn't think twice. He had simple wishes: settle a few family debts, add a room to his small house and give up the work of a sand diver as it gave him chronic cough and cold. Leaving a pregnant wife and old mother, he travelled to the Gulf after obtaining a visa from an agent, paying a huge sum of money that he had collected by taking loans from every source possible. He landed and was stranded at the airport itself, unclaimed by his job sponsor. He was grabbed by a dirty, smelly man who pushed him into the open back of his old vehicle. He faced miseries of every sort there. There are many such incidents reported these days about expats working in Gulf countries.

Anita, who worked for more than 20 years in a Gulf country, said, 'Indians used to outsmart the local bosses in the work assigned. This created insecurity in those bosses and they tried to put the expats in trouble by rating them low on performance appraisals, holding up promotions, not sending them for training, giving them mundane tasks, and some of them were sexually harassed too.'

In the globalized environment, transnational migration for work is the order of the day. The present-day employees do not tolerate a feudal work culture. They expect respect and equal treatment from their bosses.

Man, what are you searching for on the floor?

Suresh, a bank officer, resigned from his job at a nationalized bank and joined a banking company in one of the Gulf countries. He was known for his strong views in the previous organization and used to fight with the management whenever he perceived any injustice. He used to also suggest innovative strategies to the management that increased profits. Though he was perceived as a rebel, the management appreciated him for his sincerity and commitment. However, when he landed in the new job, he was in for a shock because of the dehumanizing attitude of the bosses. He adjusted to the environment, though with much difficulty. He learned to shut his mouth and became patient. He never interfered with the decisions of the management even when they were unjust, unfair or ill-conceived. One day, his boss noticed that Suresh was searching for something on the floor while leaving the office. He asked him: 'What are you searching for?' Although Suresh was searching for something that had fallen, he ended up saying something that he had wanted to tell the management for many months. 'I am searching for my self-esteem.' Suresh's sarcasm didn't go unpunished, and he had to suffer more indignation. He had to put up with it as he was worried about the Equated Monthly Instalments to the bank for his bungalow in his native town. He said, 'Many expats leave behind their self-esteem at domestic airports before taking their flights from their country.'

Salim, who worked in a Gulf country and returned for good to his native land, said, 'When I commit a genuine mistake by accident, I am verbally and physically abused by the boss. But when the same mistake was committed by a colleague from the western country, it was ignored.' Such incidents show the discrimination of bosses on the basis of certain primitive identities.

Sending those with poor cultural intelligence for offshore work

Just as bosses without cultural intelligence fail as leaders, team members with similar handicaps who work in offshore locations also tend to fail in their professional life. Though it is a fascination for many youngsters to fly to an 'advanced' foreign country, many of them go without an understanding of the work culture, lifestyle, and traditions of the new place. In many such places, these expatriate employees stay together without any effort to interact with or learn about local people and their culture. This approach can further widen the cultural and communication gap.

Thousands of highly skilled persons from India and a few other countries go to work in the US, the UK, Australia and European countries. Many bosses complain of the typical behavioural patterns of many of these expatriates. Some examples are that they:

a. Make too much noise not only when they work but also when they eat
b. Very inquisitive and gather people's personal details by directly asking them or others
c. Use resources at work for personal purposes
d. Stay put in the office after working hours and on holidays when there is no need to do so
e. Give special consideration to the people from their own region
f. Try to show respect by addressing people as 'Sir' or 'Madam' repeatedly and unnecessarily
g. Speak loudly in a language that others do not understand
h. Come late for official parties
i. Wear gaudy dresses at work

One need not necessarily be a Roman while in Rome. But one should desist from demonstrating native habits in a multicultural or foreign environment. Poor cultural intelligence could result in lack of acceptability in the organization.

Prescription for you, the boss

There is no justification for your xenophobic attitude if you decide to have an expat in your organization. If you cannot treat the person without discrimination due to your perception that he is lacking in competence, communication and other skills, it is better not to hire him.

Precaution for you

Be aware of the professional, social and cultural environment of the country you are going to work in. Don't be aggressive and confrontational even for apparently justifiable reasons. One needs to air grievances through established channels within organizations or to trustworthy senior colleagues.

Precept for the organization

Induction training for new recruits from other cultures should not be routine or one-sided. Cultural awareness should be extended to the bosses as well in order to help them understand expat team members better. Create an environment where employees are encouraged to share what they feel to a responsible functionary within the organization.

The signs of recovery

No expats will be conscious or worried about being in a different culture in organizations that treat them equally. Rather, perfect acculturation would result in the feeling that they are expats in their native culture!

Please assess your Cultural Intelligence Score if you work or plan to work in a different cultural setting.

Exercise 3

What is your Cultural Intelligence score?

(Mark your responses below or in a separate sheet)

1. When you go to stay in a new place, do you take interest in learning about the history, culture and traditions of that place?
   a. I do not take any interest
   b. That is not my priority, but I will if I am exposed to it
   c. I try to ask others to know more
   d. I make deliberate efforts to learn by observing
   e. I collect data from the local library, internet, and archives
2. I am proud of my own cultural traditions and the background I was brought up in, therefore
   a. I am always excited to learn from better cultural traditions if I come across them
   b. I respect other cultures as well
   c. I don't find other cultures and traditions superior to mine

d. I do not wish to get assimilated with any culture
   e. I passionately spread my cultural traditions in the new place and point out the shortcomings in theirs
3. When I see people following a diet that is totally against the dietary practices of the culture in which I was brought up, I
   a. try to correct them
   b. try to move away from them
   c. am not interested in knowing what they eat
   d. try to know more about their dietary habits
   e. try to understand the benefits of their diet
4. When I need to interact at work with people from unfamiliar countries or regions, I
   a. try to get familiarized with the communication tools and techniques acceptable to them
   b. follow the prevalent communication pattern at work without making an extra effort
   c. familiarize them with the communication tools and techniques that I am used to
   d. make it clear to them that I can't change the way I have been communicating
   e. avoid all situations at work where I need to interact with them
5. Which is your most preferred kind of boss out of the following?
   a. A person from my own region
   b. A person who shares my religious faith
   c. A person who understands my language
   d. A person who understands my emotions and expectations
   e. A person whose emotions and expectations I can understand
6. Which is your most preferred team member out of the following?
   a. A person from my own region
   b. A person who shares my religious faith
   c. A person who understands my language
   d. A person who understands my emotions and expectations
   e. A person whose emotions and expectations I can understand

7. Do you
   a. know many (more than three) languages other than your native language?
   b. know at least one foreign language?
   c. like to learn more languages if provided an opportunity?
   d. prefer to take the help of a translator rather than learning a new language?
   e. prefer to work in an environment where the majority speak a language you know
8. Do you
   a. make deliberate efforts to understand the body language and verbal expressions of others in the new cultural setting and try to emulate what you find appropriate?
   b. take deliberate efforts to understand the body language and verbal expressions of others in the new cultural setting and try to emulate them?
   c. take deliberate efforts to understand the body language and verbal expressions of others in the new cultural setting and compare yours?
   d. prefer not to bother about understanding the body language and verbal expressions of others in the new cultural setting?
   e. hate to understand the body language and verbal expressions of others in the new cultural setting?
9. Do you
   a. feel happy when you attend an ethnic gathering in the host community where you are invited and you don't understand the language or customs and were given food you are not used to?
   b. take the above as an opportunity to learn about the host culture?
   c. tolerate the above though you don't really enjoy it?
   d. try to leave the place after making a quick appearance?
   e. refuse any such invitation?

10. Do you
   a. recognize the inherent inequality among various categories of people in the host culture and orient your actions and behaviour in accordance with the special treatment given by the government of that country to backward categories?
   b. try to understand the inherent inequality between various social groups living in the host culture and orient your actions and behaviour in accordance with the special treatment given by the government of that country to backward categories?
   c. ignore any such inequality or treatment as stated above in your action and behaviour?
   d. feel that you are not concerned about such people and the inequalities in that country?
   e. hate special treatments given to any group by the government of that country?

Please go to page 257 to see a quick analysis of your score.

©Sibichen K. Mathew

44

THE BEST LEAVE; THE WORST STAY

A PUBLIC SECTOR banking company faced a fall in its net income due to huge salary pay-outs. The new boss, who claimed to be a master strategist, was at the head of the committee that looked into the financials. He suggested a 'Voluntary Retirement Scheme' (VRS), which, aiming for a reduction of about 30 per cent of personnel, provided an attractive monetary compensation package for those who resigned. The scheme was successful, with about 35 per cent of manpower taking up the offer. The company was happy, but realized its mistake very soon. It had lost all the best employees through the scheme, since they knew they could walk into another company with their competency levels. Those who stayed back in the company were mostly shirkers, idlers or the untrained ones who would not get similar opportunities elsewhere. Instead of an aggressive and unprofessional VRS, the company headed by the new 'strategic' boss should have focused on measures that would help identify and retain the best employees.

Gone are the days when people work for one particular company for many years. Today, information on better pastures is available at people's fingertips due to the influential and wide-reaching existence of social networking platforms and other online sources. People decide to leave organizations and join new ones within a few hours or days. Even when there is a recession or large-scale unemployment, there is always a market for the best employees. The greatest challenge for organizations is to find out how to tackle high attrition rates.

In a study[119] conducted by Hudson Institute and Walker Information in 1999 on employees of private, government and non-governmental organizations in the US, it was found that one in four employees (24 per cent) is considered 'Truly Loyal' to the organization (employee is committed to the organization and plans to stay for two years), one in three employees (33 per cent) is considered 'High Risk' (employee is not committed to the organization and does not plan to stay for the next two years) and four in 10 employees (39 per cent) are 'Trapped' (employee is not committed to the organization, but plans on staying at the organization for the next two years). Similar trends may be seen in many organizations across the world.

'If you give peanuts, you will get only monkeys'. This famous saying is attributed to French businessman, politician, and publisher, Sir James Goldsmith. A white paper presented by the Government of Singapore in 1994 endorsed this view, stating, 'If you give peanuts you will get monkeys for your ministers. The people will suffer, not the monkeys.' It is not just a hefty salary; employees also want a hassle-free work environment that gives opportunities to grow professionally. In the absence of that, they may suffer from lethargy, low productivity and lack of ambition. Those who want to demonstrate their professional competence look elsewhere for better opportunities. Those who want to enjoy the comfortable life continue in the same organization. Over a period of time, a bunch of zombies can be observed in the organization, mostly at lower and middle levels. Since they have become incompetent and not in demand, they stay on. They are unaffected by schemes like the VRS.

Three groups of zombies in the public sector

Government organizations usually have a larger share of zombies. Broadly, there are three groups of people in government. Those in the first set (the large group) have entered the ivory tower for comfort and so-called security. The second group (a smaller group) wants to be creative and constructive. The third set thinks it would be the best business option. All the above categories thrive initially. Then, the first group has to contend with the peanuts. The second group slowly realize that they are in an iron cage where they can't do much. They are affected by 'learned helplessness'. The brighter ones from the group crave for a suitable opportunity to get out to follow their dreams. The third set of people continue to take risks and use their powerful energy for sucking in beyond what is due to them, so as to extend their empire. Even with this ill-gotten abundance they believe they are affected by the 'peanut syndrome' and long for what they don't yet have.

Attrition is a symptom of malignancy

Mindtree, the global IT solution company, had an attrition rate of 25 per cent at one point of time. Though one study (chartered by the company itself) attributes it to 'improper communication,'[120] the truth points towards the salaries. The company is happy with those who have happily stayed back with less pay. But what about competence? Worldcom faced a terrible situation due to unethical practices triggered by inefficient accounting and audits. It is said that it had only half the number of executives in its accounting wing as compared to several other telecommunication companies of equal or lesser size.[121] It was also reported that the internal auditors were paid very low salaries.

It was Barry Gibbons, former CEO of Burger King, who said that 'people are coin-operated'. If you give peanuts, you will definitely get many monkeys. If you continue to give peanuts for long, some may still work like donkeys, very quietly and sincerely, though their cerebral cortex would be in a dormant state. However, what should worry bosses more is why the best employees are leaving the organization in spite of giving them 'cookies'.

The leaving employee is not an enemy

It is not a bad thing to look for better opportunities and people do that often if there is scope. The organization should not regard the leaving employee as an enemy. Many employees suffer because of the unnecessary bottlenecks created at the time of their departure. Many of them were the best contributors in the company; do not give them an opportunity to tarnish the image of the organization wherever they go next. Exit interviews can be of great help since employees who leave can freely air their views; the data gathered, compiled and tracked over time can be used for improvement.

Prescription for you, the boss

Don't take the brighter ones in your team for granted. Pamper them if needed by giving them the best that they deserve for their competency.

Precaution for you

There is not much you can do here, other than look for a better opportunity if you are sure that your happiness lies elsewhere.

Precept for the organization

There is no single strategy to retain the best in the organization. Frequent one-to-one interactions of the boss with team members can bring in information about the career goals of the latter. Bosses can find out the points of dissatisfaction before they get a surprise. It is necessary to find out why a consistent performer might be indifferent or slipping in his work.

If the organization charges more for the best of the products, why not pay well for the best employees, rather than looking at his years of experience or position in the organizational hierarchy?

The signs of recovery

No one would leave an organization that nurtures, recognizes and fulfils the core needs of a person in modern society, that is builds his self-esteem—the feeling that he is valuable for people.

45

BOSS IS FROM MARS; YOU ARE FROM VENUS

SARA, THE EXECUTIVE Assistant to the CEO of an MNC in Bangalore, was a primary witness to how acculturation problems can create havoc in an organization. In order to bring up the company, whose turnover had dipped in recent years, the US headquarters relocated Mr Smith, an American citizen from Washington, to replace the Indian CEO. For Smith, this was his first expatriate assignment; he had not been to India even as a tourist. Due to this, he could not adjust with the work culture. He would get furious when he saw team members sticking to their own schedule in spite of clearly laid out work timings. He was astonished to see people spending time on personal calls and social networking sites during office hours. He issued warning letters to those who used to come late in the office. He ordered the system administrator to block websites on the wifi network so that executives and managers wouldn't use company resources to browse data on their smartphones. More than any of this, he was very irritated by the loud conversations at work stations.

Senior managers could not tolerate the restrictions imposed on them. They said, 'What if we come late to office sometimes because of personal emergencies? Don't we sit late in the office to clear all the tasks? What if we are on social networking sites while at office? Has that affected our output? How many Saturdays have we come and worked?' Sara tried to convince Smith about the work culture in the organization and the commitment of the team. But he was not ready to listen. He just asked her to look at the result sheet of the organization.

D.A. Victor has identified two types of cultures:[122] Monochronic culture and polychronic culture. Some of the several attributes of monochronic culture as identified by him are: a) interpersonal relations are subordinate to the present schedule, b) rigid appointment time, c) one task at a time, d) work time is clearly separable from personal time, and e) tasks are measured by output in time. On the contrary, the attributes of polychronic culture include: a) the present schedule is subordinate to interpersonal relations, b) flexible appointment time, c) multi-tasking, d) work time is not clearly separable from personal time, and e) tasks are measured as part of an overall organizational goal. One can identify countries with monochronic and polychronic cultures on the basis of attitudes towards work and the social and cultural traditions and approaches within each country. There are substantial variations between regions.

Globalization, undoubtedly, has created fresh cultural and communication challenges within organizations. In a globalized work environment, one would find bosses and team members from various regional, ethnic and linguistic backgrounds. Wibbeke, a scholar of business leadership, has said that a leader who can accommodate and master the problems related to leading a multi-cultural workforce can be said to have mastered what he called 'Geoleadership'.[123] With proper guidance and training, organizations can create a workforce that can assimilate people and their cultures without compromising on the organizational culture, vision and goals.

Bosses lacking in cultural intelligence

In a globalized and technology-driven work environment, people need cultural intelligence. This is nothing but sense and sensibility around the social and cultural contexts of the people living in a particular geographic space. It need not be an insistence to learn the language, but respecting the language. It is not about following particular customs but about not being prejudicial. It is not about showing laxity or tolerating indiscipline but about being sensitive to genuine social requirements. Realizing the importance of demands placed by increasing cross-cultural interactions, many schools of etiquette have sprung up. Before going abroad to work, it is advisable to be aware of the expected code of behaviour in the new workplace and social settings. Business etiquette is as important as social etiquette.

Some of the attributes of cultural intelligence are:

- Willingness to learn about the new cultural setting one is in
- Understanding the essential ingredients of the new culture
- Absence of ethnocentrism (a view or feeling that your own culture is far superior to the new culture you are in)
- Not being judgemental
- Not having prejudice and stereotypical notions
- Understanding that organizations have many other functional roles apart from maximizing revenue
- Being aware that people work to fulfil not only economic needs but also sociological needs
- Becoming familiar with the local etiquette

In an increasingly cross-cultural work environment, there could be several other areas where bosses or team members need to have 'cultural awareness'.

Intercultural leadership competencies

A successful leader is one who makes deliberate efforts to cultivate competencies that can make him acceptable in and compatible with diverse cultures. While preserving one's own culture, no one should forget the reality of a global village where people, organizations and governments necessarily work together.

In a study[124] conducted by Eileen Sheridan on intercultural leadership competencies of US business leaders, the following competencies were identified by a sample of intercultural communication experts at different levels. In the intrapersonal dimension, seven competencies were identified: a) self-awareness, b) flexibility/adaptability, c) curiosity, d) patience, e) ambiguity tolerance, f) mindfulness and g) imagination. In the interpersonal dimensions, two competencies were identified: a) perspective taking and b) non-judgemental. In social dimensions, competencies such as a) effective communication, b) sensitivity/appreciation of difference, c) local-global perspective, d) understanding how leadership is conceptualized in other cultures, and e) multi-lingual, were identified.

Tony worked as a senior manager in a multinational company in India and quit out of frustration. He said, 'Indian managers are slaves of foreign bosses. The company "XBM" where I was working earlier suddenly brought a person from "XCS" to be in charge of the global delivery, by paying him five times his earlier salary. The mandate given to him was to bring in the tight financial regime followed in XCS to XBM. He started doing so by cutting additional incentives for employees. Recovery charges were brought down from 25 dollars to 10 dollars; these changes helped the foreign company to make money. Many middle-level managers left the company because of the higher stress. XCS had several good work practices for employee welfare and employee retention, but none of them got transplanted in XBM.'

What was wrong with the policy of XBM? It rapidly transplanted a culture to a completely different setting without proper homework. This resulted in dissatisfaction and discontent in the organization.

Author in conversation with Marten Pieters

Being a boss in a new culture and context

How was your experience of working in a different socio-cultural environment as compared to your earlier positions in other countries?
- There is no definite gospel to be accepted in a new country: an open mind, understanding the environment and people, drawing parallels from previous experience, building local talent and processes, and having a long-term view rather than short-term

delivery builds trust in the organization. I am in India right now. I found that India has a very rich and diverse culture and to do business here, it is extremely important that you understand the uniqueness of the geographic, socio-economic and cultural diversity here. I feel that all leaders, when they go to a new culture, should be ready to learn something new.

What are the challenges in assimilating the local plans and flavours with the big picture?
- One should understand the unique cultural, social and political background and dynamics in the country before venturing to formulate and implement policies and projects. When you lead a team in a new culture or area, understanding the existing strategy and structure and reframing them to get optimum results are the biggest tasks at hand. My task, when I started my work in India, was delicate: preserve the entrepreneurial spirit that had become inherent to the company, while drawing a big picture and inculcating a greater sense of logic to decision-making. India may be one country, but it is almost as many markets as Europe. Each one has a different competitive situation, a different customer profile. You need local plans and flavours to approach each market.

According to you, what are the attributes required for a leader to succeed in a new culture?
- In my opinion, a successful leader has to be open and accommodating. It is necessary that the person is able to embrace the country's culture, drive the direction of the business and yet demonstrate an exactness in being process-driven. He has to be nimble in his decision-making, and enable freedom and empowerment down the line. Understanding the market by listening to your customers is the basis for a successful commercial strategy. Listening to your employees is the first step to a successful implementation of the strategy.

How did you cope with the cross-cultural challenges within the organization?
- It is interesting to see that when I came in and started out with a more democratic management style, it was not really working and was confusing for my team members. Where that would work well in most European countries, and even in Africa, it did not work in India. People were looking for clear instructions and a clear direction. So I adjusted my style to that, and then relaxed it again over time, expecting more independence from my team members and more delegation of tasks. I believe we now have a less central decision-making process than when I came; managers are more relaxed about delegation of authority and are willing to take that responsibility.

Mr Pieters is one of the most successful CEOs of his time. He started his career in Royal Smilde Food NY, worked in various capacities with companies such as KPN in the US, Eastern Europe and Asia, and later moved to Celtel International. Subsequently he joined as the CEO of Vodafone-India.

46

IS THE FAMILY THE SHOCK ABSORBER OR THE SHOCK TRIGGER?

MOST OF US spend a substantial part of our life in the organizations in which we work. A person who starts from his house for an eight-hour schedule of work may spend a considerable amount of time in travelling to and from office. Thus, if a person spends more than 10 hours outside his house every day, the time spent with the family, excluding the time to sleep, would be much less. Nevertheless, life and relationships within the four corners of one's house are more meaningful and crucial for many.

Tina was very happy when she got a job at a prestigious research centre. After completing her PhD in biomedical engineering, a project under a renowned researcher was a dream came true for her. However, within a few days of working under the scientist, she was miserable. She found the boss to be very demanding, cold and inconsiderate. She carried home her unpleasant experiences every day and shared these with her husband. She got up every day with a deep ache, worrying about the work on that day. A bright student and a passionate researcher, she started hating her job. How long could this continue? The husband was also equally perturbed and tension began to mount at home, so much so that their relationship was affected. Their strategies didn't work. Finally, unable to see light at the end of the tunnel, Tina quit her dream job.

Nobody can tolerate such a situation for a very long time. There can be instances where people fight with such bosses, resulting in the loss of their jobs. Restubog, Scott and Zagenczyk have found that aggressive norms and consequent aggressive behaviour of bosses may have negative ramifications for employees and their families. Tensions can develop at home due to the strains generated at the workplace.

Working from home

There is an increasing trend of allowing employees to work from home. Some like it, but some don't. Those who want to get away from the family do not like to engage in office work at home. But in a study[125] conducted by Nicholas Bloom and his student at Stanford University, it was found that employees who were allowed to work from home were not only happier and less likely to quit, but also more productive.

Praying for the boss's wife

I heard this at a coffee outlet: 'I pray to God for the boss's wife every day. Let her not wake up today in a bad mood!' When the jeans-clad young man shared this fervent plea, the elderly one in the group commented, 'I pray for the news that our boss has divorced that cranky lady.' They were discussing how the mood of their boss is determined by the mood of his wife at home. The driver who collects the lunch box of the boss from the 'boss madam' would clearly know the mood of that day. He would promptly alert the team: 'Be ready for the blasts today!'

In a study conducted by C. Binnewies et al.[126] it was found that being highly relaxed in the morning is related to increased task performance and helpful behaviour during the day. They also found that for people with a high level of job control, the relationship between being relaxed and daily performance was stronger.

When shock transmits to the family

Most team members avoid reacting to an irritable boss since they don't want to lose their job or fear disciplinary action. Some suffer patiently, waiting for a change of boss. However, there are bosses who direct their anger towards others. Marcus-Newhall et al.[127] found that in such situations, the aggression is likely to be shifted from the original focal point to other targets. Abused and humiliated employees might take their anger out on family members, further aggravating their agony.

In a family get together, there was an interesting sharing session by the spouses of senior managers in various organizations. Each person was asked to narrate how the work environment of the spouse created health problems for the spouse and consequent strains in the family. In an era where so much is being talked about marital breakdowns because of ego and selfishness in couples, the feedback given by the spouses was quite revealing. Most of them said that the strains that occur in the family are direct results of the strains suffered at the workplace and especially from immediate bosses. If the spouse comes home and heads straight to bed, to the club or to the cricket match rather than chatting, it is probably because of the tensions he carries from office that cannot be shared with the family, as it might spoil their mood too. But the partners might think that the spouse is ignoring them.

℞ Prescription for you, the boss

Making the team aware of family strains through your moods, expressions or sharing may result in letting them see you in poor light. This could in turn erode your credibility and your image. Instead of gaining respect, you would end up getting sympathy.

Precaution for you

It is good to share your experiences with your spouse at home. In any case, partners are there for mutual support in times of need. By all means, unburden yourself; however, do so within limits. They might get fed up listening to your woes all the time. Taking out anger generated at work on your family is useless.

Precept for the organization

There is not much you can do, other than encouraging informal networks, recreation centres and counselling facilities at the office.

The signs of recovery

When organizations assist their employees in maintaining a healthy and satisfying work-family balance, they get commitment and loyalty in return.

Exercise 4

Ask and assess yourself

How much do the events and situations in your family and personal life impact your performance at work?

How much do the events and situations at work impact your personal and family life?

47

DON'T COUNT JUST THE SUCCESSES; COUNT THE TEARS TOO

LEE IACOCCA TURNED Chrysler around when it was on the verge of collapse, when he took the unprecedented step of taking a loan guarantee from the government. But he was accused of being authoritarian as he made decisions without considering the feedback from others below him. Alan Mulally rescued Ford from near bankruptcy, but was criticized for his aggressive leadership style. Steve Jobs was one of the greatest technological innovators of recent times. He built Apple and led it to the top. But many who worked under him perceived him as arrogant, not transparent and abrasive.

There are many successful bosses who bring laurels to the organizations through their dynamic and daring leadership. However, most people forget that glory is built on the tears of many. Organizations succeeded. A few received accolades. But there would be some who had to face insults, torture, harassment, humiliation or threats. Organizations can succeed with bosses who lack emotional intelligence but are high in intellectual capability. Every successful boss can be a successful manager. But he may not be a successful leader.

Mr Verma was the head of an autonomous establishment in the government. He was a person with a clear vision and mission for the organization and worked hard to create a space for the organization internationally. He made even the laziest employees work hard and monitored progress every now and then. He made everyone sit late in office and extracted work. As a result of his efforts, output doubled during his term. At the same time, during the journey to success, many in the organization felt that they were kicked, pushed and insulted.

Leader first, manager next

Why are many team members happy when their manager is on leave, just like the absence of teachers brings cheer to the students? If managers are hated, can't we get rid of them altogether? Morning Star, the world's largest tomato processor, claims that their 'managerless' model has been functioning successfully for the last 20 years. It allows employees to manage themselves. In an analysis of the company,[128] Glary Hamel concluded that companies of any size can emulate this model. It is possible that organizations survive without managers, but not without leaders!

The question 'Managers and leaders: are they different?' has been asked by scholars since the 1970s. The term 'manager' has become out-of-date. David Chard, president, Engaging Minds Worldwide wrote, 'It doesn't mean we should eliminate all managers; rather we should teach our managers how to lead'.[129] Abraham Zaleznik[130] argued that the scientific management theories of leadership have ignored the inspiration, vision and full spectrum of human drives and desires. He was critical of the highly rational, utilitarian and scientific approaches to study leadership. Management theorist and scholar John P. Kotter suggested an approach that considers management and leadership as distinctive but complementary systems of action. Both are necessary for a dynamic organization. In his article, 'What leaders really do?'[131] Kotter leaves the function of 'planning' also to the manager so that the leader can focus on setting direction. He says, 'Planning is a management process, deductive in nature and designed to produce orderly results, not change. Setting a direction is more inductive.' Thus, leaders create vision and strategies.

All good leaders are not good managers. Similarly, all good managers are not good leaders. A perfect manager is the one who is also a good leader. Some characteristic traits that make them distinct are:

Manager	Leader
Implementer	Motivator
Co-ordinator	Planner
Organizer	Thinker
Rule-bound	Visionary
Examiner	Evaluator
Target-oriented	Proactive
Focuses on output	Focuses on outcome
Supervisor	Guide
Invests in the best team members	Invests to improve the weak members
Aims at short-term benefits	Aims at long-term benefits
Task-oriented	Relations-oriented
Thinks they are indispensable	Nurtures new leaders

Strategies of egocentric managers who think they are indispensable

1. No delegation
2. No one given a road map
3. Do not define the responsibilities of subordinates
4. Deliberately create confusion
5. Plant bottlenecks
6. Demand vetting at every stage
7. Directions come in trickles. Leave gaps.
8. Distribute work in parts to different persons. No one knows the whole picture.

We need bosses with integrated traits

A truly successful boss acts as a leader as well as a manager. He wears both hats with ease. The theoretical premise of the famous Performance-Maintenance Leadership theory that 'effective leaders are high in both performance behaviour and maintenance behaviour' is very much relevant here. The leader should be a team-builder, facilitator and a stimulator of ideas. In a very real sense, leadership is a journey from the head to the heart. A judicious mix of intellect and emotion is what a leader should display. A powerful leader is not the one who exercises maximum power over the people, but one who has a positive influence on the team. Mary Parker Follet, a pioneer in organizational theory and organizational behaviour, emphasized that leaders should have 'power with' and not 'power over' workers.

When leaders become mentors

It is often said that we need leaders and not managers. Successful leaders need to go one step further than managers. When one is in charge of a fairly responsible and dedicated team that has the urge to excel further, the leader takes the role of a mentor. The differences in attributes between leader and mentor, though some of them are not mutually exclusive, are:

Leader	Mentor
Voluntariness is not predominant	Voluntariness is predominant
Looks at end result	Looks at growth
Role director	Role model
Provides the road map	Facilitates to create the road map
Active and continuous monitoring	Interferes and evaluates only when requested
Leaders do not choose the team	Mentors choose the mentees
Suited for large groups	Suited for small groups
Trusted for capability	Trusted more for the experience
Shows the way	Trains and counsels to select the way
Leaders and followers need not be mutually committed	Mentors and mentees are always mutually committed
Very much an insider	Could be an outsider
Larger role in selecting the space, time and nature	Space, time and nature depend on the preferences of mentee

48

THE CORPORATE BUREAUCRATIC BOSSES AND EMOTIONAL INTELLIGENCE

GOVERNMENTS THE WORLD over follow an assertion attributed to Margaret Thatcher: 'The government should not be in the business of doing business.' It is left to the private sector to cater to the needs of people, whether it is trading, manufacturing or the service sector. The last several decades have seen a consolidation of business activities in the hands of a few large corporates and they have emerged as market leaders employing thousands of people and catering to millions of customers. This has created massive structures of decision-making within the companies, with clearly defined hierarchies. Leadership, people management and customer service have taken a different dimension with much more impersonality, complexity and technicality.

For many years, we blamed the government and government organizations for being inefficient, complex, and corrupt. We adored Max Weber for appropriately applying the word 'bureaucracy' and spoiled the meaning of this nomenclature by attributing it to anyone and anything that is adamant, stoic, apathetic or irresponsive. Inevitable regulatory systems imprisoned government officials inside an iron cage while giving them peanuts. They were asked to perform with their hands tied to their backs. A similar situation is being witnessed in large private organizations where the employees are hired and fired at will, pay and recognition are given on subjective considerations and decisions are marred by bottlenecks.

George was a senior manager with several years of experience in a large company. He maintained a cordial relationship with his team members, vendors, suppliers and other stakeholders. He spent his evenings with his wife and two daughters chatting, watching movies and having a relaxed dinner with them. However, everything changed after Khan took over as his boss. Khan was well known in the industry for his technical competence and successful implementation of a business process flow that reduced delays and ensured higher efficiency. Working under him, George learnt to be more ambitious. He understood the need for not just achieving profits but also making the company a global leader by moving ahead of competitors. He realized that one needs to be tough with mediocre employees, and slow learners should be fired. Stiff targets forced him to be harsh with creditors. Ultimately, he achieved his targets and got an elevation, but his life was not the same. He was rarely with his family for their daily quality time. He found that his blood pressure and cholesterol levels had reached dangerous levels.

The experiences of the other employees were no different under the aggressive strategic leadership of Khan and the same was the case of other stakeholders of the company. Suppliers felt intense pressure to deliver in spite of difficulties. The customers were up in arms because the company had cut short the period of credit and reduced discounts. The company's profits soared but were not sustainable. After a while, Khan conveniently left the company with another feather in his cap. Profits plummeted as some of the regular suppliers and long-standing customers switched allegiance. It also lost some loyal and committed employees.

What was the reason for the sharp fall? What was wrong with the strategies and style of functioning of the leader? How did a technocrat, an alumnus of a premier institute of technology and a top school of management, not secure enduring profits for the company? Why were all stakeholders unhappy with his policies?

The answer is simple. The technocrat failed to understand and deal with the sociological context within which the organization and business worked. Stiff targets, aggressive strategies and rigid business conditions can force people to act and respond beyond their normal capability and potential only for a while. Organizations change their culture based on the ideologies and values they uphold. Why do team members feel so unimportant in the system in large private organizations? This is because: a) The profit motive is more predominant than the service motive, b) The tendency is to sub-contract the work to make more profit and consequent lack of loyalty to the organization, c) there is high attrition among the employees and lack of long-term commitment, d) Lower risks for mischief-makers as they can vanish from the company before being caught and punished, and e) When company practices are perceived to be unethical, the employees also tend to become dishonest and selfish.

In the above scenario, where the sole driving force of bosses is to achieve targets at any cost, there would be less emphasis on fairness and empathy.

Rational organizations and suppressed emotions

Man is an emotional being. There are a large number of emotional responses generated within every individual every day in response to what he sees, hears and experiences. A man without emotions is as good as a corpse. No element of professionalism and rational thinking can allow for the neglect of emotions of people and their aspirations and expectations. Though no boss should tolerate uncontrolled manifestation of emotions by anyone in the organization, he cannot totally ignore the feelings of people working at different levels. Several studies indicate that bosses who are empathetic and responsive to employees' needs are particularly successful in managing their emotional reactions.[132]

In order to understand others better, bosses need to have the right capabilities and competencies. They should look at people, beyond spreadsheets and graphs. Apart from cognitive intelligence, bosses need to have high emotional intelligence.

Goleman argued that emotional intelligence matters more than IQ.[133] Emotional intelligence helps in balancing and regulating emotional responses such as anger, fear, happiness and demonstration of affection. It aids in understanding the emotional responses and needs of others. Goleman has rightly observed that emotional intelligence is a construct that represents a constellation of traits and abilities that are not fully explored in the traditional measures of personality. After studying leadership in 188 companies, he calculated the ratio of technical skills, IQ and emotional intelligence as being the ingredients of excellent performance, and found that emotional intelligence is twice as important as the others for jobs at all levels.[134]

Robert B. Denhardt and Janet V. Denhardt[135] said, 'The act of leading results in a flow of human energy in a particular direction and at a particular speed and tempo.' The scholars, by looking at the world of art, music and especially dance, were able to identify certain key elements of the art of leadership. They say that leadership touches the human spirit, and touching the human spirit has always been the work of art and aesthetics. Thus, one must learn leadership from acting as a leader. According to Debasis, 'leadership is not a science or an art, it is a state of consciousness in which we discover the path to our own kingdoms.'[136]

Organizations need to develop leaders with the above skills. They can focus on the behavioural and emotional dimensions only by creating small, independent and responsible units within the existing structures. Each unit should be delegated powers based on unique attributes and should be accountable for its operational decisions. Technological interface should not undermine the genuine need for human interaction to find satisfying solutions to problems. For this, we need to go back to the concept of 'Small is Beautiful' to get rid of the ghost of Max Weber and his iron-caged bureaucracy.

What is your Emotional Intelligence Score (EQ-i)?

Only a 360-degree analysis based on feedback from you, your colleagues, subordinates, superiors, and others would give a clear picture of your EQ-i. One needs to respond to questions on interpersonal skills, intra-personal skills, adaptability, stress management and general mood (actual and not perceived or desirable). There are many standardized tests to assess emotional intelligence.[137] Organizations need to adopt such measures.

You can assess your emotional intelligence by taking the test on page 260.

Exercise 5

Boss, what is your level of emotional intelligence?

A person with emotional intelligence can understand one's own emotional status as well that of others. He can manage emotions successfully, get relieved from stress, understand the communication of others, effectively communicate to them, empathize with others, resolve conflicts, balance his emotions and maintain relationships. There are several standardized measurements to check the emotional intelligence score (EQ-i). Given below is a simple questionnaire not to accurately measure your emotional intelligence, but to create awareness of your strengths and areas of competency on various aspects of emotional intelligence. Questions and statements are presented to you based on the five-element framework of emotional intelligence as delineated by Daniel Golman. They are a) Self-Awareness, b) Self-Regulation, c) Motivation, d) Empathy and e) Social Skills.

(Questions and statements given below are in the context of a 'boss' and based on the themes discussed in this book. The objective is to provide a general idea of various attributes of emotional intelligence and not to arrive at a particular score. Readers are advised to undergo standardized and comprehensive testing with a 360-degree feedback from all persons around to arrive at a correct score.)

Please answer imagining that you were in the situations mentioned in the statements, irrespective of whether you have really faced these or not. Be honest in your reply to get the correct assessment. Give your response (A,B,C,D or E) in the box given at the right side of each statement or in a separate sheet. (A—Definitely; B—Very likely; C—likely; D—less likely; E—never)

1. When you find that an employee has acted contrary to what you have advised in the best interest of that person, you will immediately confront him rather than postponing your angry response. ☐
2. If your manager down the line did not update you about the progress of the project though you had directed him to do so, instead of getting annoyed you would politely ask for the progress report. ☐
3. Imagine a situation when you become very critical of the performance of the team in a meeting and strongly express your unhappiness about the poor results. Would you feel displeased if a few team members express their dissent and criticized the management for the poor results? ☐
4. Even when you are in an extremely bad mood because of certain personal issues, you would hold the meeting with your team at the scheduled time though you have the power to postpone it. ☐
5. You like this employee for his excellent output, sincerity and devotion to work. But he tends to bypass the established procedures which everyone expected to follow. You don't mind condoning the procedural lapses since he is one of your favourite employees. ☐
6. If your boss has shouted at you for something your team is responsible and that has emotionally disturbed you, will you show your anger immediately to the team? ☐
7. When a manager down the line comes to you and narrates an incident of indiscipline by an employee, you would take action against the employee instantly rather than delaying it. ☐
8. There are instances in the past when you over-reacted in meetings, causing unpleasant situations ☐
9. You would reject any suggestion from the team after the project design is finalized and the time to give suggestions has elapsed. ☐

10. When the project is in the final stage, your boss tells you to change the design or strategy, which would mean severe strains on the team. You would get demotivated to continue. ☐
11. When you came to know that an order has been issued in respect of the posting under you of a manager who was chucked out from another division for indiscipline and inefficiency, you will express your protest with your boss immediately. ☐
12. If a customer directly barges into your room with a genuine complaint when you are busy with your work, you would get annoyed and ask him to meet the concerned manager concerned. ☐
13. You convened a meeting of the entire team and concerned with the fast approaching deadline of the project, instructed them to strictly adhere to the timings. If you noticed that one manager continued to come late to office, you would immediately take action against him for disobedience. ☐
14. After detailed thought and analysis, you took a decision. However, a team member gave a totally different suggestion, which was made without any understanding of the situation. You will not waste time analysing the rationale of that suggestion. ☐
15. An employee, though reasonably intelligent, has very poor pronunciation and language skills. In important meetings where top bosses attend, you ensure that the employee, in order to avoid any embarrassment, doesn't get enough opportunities to speak. ☐
16. Your successor gets an award for a job substantially done by you. In your congratulatory speech you would highlight your contributions to the work. ☐
17. You have a special affection and obligation towards those team members who greeted you with flowers and gifts on your birthday than those who didn't. ☐
18. You greet back with a smile to the security guard and sweepers every day when you reach office just like you reciprocate the

greetings of the senior employees. ☐

19. If there is an unsettled issue or communication gap between any of the colleagues, you will call both parties to give a fair judgement and settle the issues. ☐

20. Your team got selected as the best performing unit and was nominated for an award. But you found out that the judges committed an error in awarding higher marks to your team. Actually, the award should have gone to some other team. No one is aware of the goof up. You would choose to keep it under wraps and would not bring it to the notice of the management. ☐

For a quick assessment of your emotional intelligence, go to page 258.

©Sibichen K. Mathew

49

STATIC RULES AND ROCKY BOSSES

IT IS BELIEVED by the faithful that the 'Ten Commandments' is the result of infinite wisdom and it is 'theopneustos' (Latin word, meaning God-breathed). So are several other sacred texts of various religious denominations. For this reason, the rules given by them are considered infallible, unamendable and perennially applicable. I prefer not to sit in judgement about these beliefs. But this can't

be true in respect of the rules within mundane organizations that comprise people and related social embeddedness. Can the rules governing the rights, duties, privileges, conduct and prospects of team members within an organization be static and permanent, in spite of the social, economic, technological and behavioural changes over a period of time? Dissatisfaction and conflict emerge and prevail in many organizations because of the reluctance to amend rules in accordance with the changing conditions and requirements. They fail to grasp the fact that old gives way to the new.

Here is an example of a public sector organization. There was a rule that allowed reimbursement of medical claims for emergency medical surgeries in private hospitals. The employee was eligible for reimbursement of the amount from the employer with a cap, for example, of 50 dollars for an appendicitis surgery in accordance with a very archaic rule. But the heads of office were given the necessary powers to increase or decrease the reimbursement based on the actual cost and its reasonableness. The organization maintained this rule for many decades so the employees would get only 50 dollars even when the cost in private hospitals had increased manifold. Most of the bosses didn't bother to align the rule to the changing times.

'You show me the man; I will show you the rule'. This is an oft-repeated statement in many organizations that flout rules to satisfy specific interests. Here the rule is flexible and to be bent at convenience, or interpreted to suit specific needs.

An executive of a large corporate house shared this: 'We had an outdated Standard Operating Procedure for choosing vendors. This had diluted the process and we were not shortlisting the right ones. Though I pointed this out to the boss several times, he was not ready to listen. He said: "I can't change radically something which has been in practice for many years. Let my successor do it if he wants."'

Individuals within an organization, though preserving their unique identities, tend to find meaning in their interactions with each other. They also prefer to be in communication with friends and relations who physically exist outside the organizational network.

People have expectations and interests and they orient their actions to fulfil their desires. However, if organizational rules do not permit a relational structure desired by individuals, dissatisfaction arises. Thus there is a conflict between the rule-based actions and choice-based actions. In organizations, choice-based actions by individuals invite criticism, disciplinary action or even termination, depending upon the amount of deviation from the rules. Rule-based actions have been analysed by many prominent scholars from the field of sociology, such as Durkheim[138] and Merton.[139] James G. March, Martin Schulz, and Xueguang Zhou studied the dynamics of rules in formal organizational settings through an empirical study.[140]

Modern organizations have business rules at three levels: One, with reference to the external stakeholders such as customers and the public. Second, the rules that govern internal functions to perform tasks for the external stakeholders. Third, the rules that govern the relationships and conduct of persons within the organizations. Though the third one, which is more personal in nature, cannot be called business rules, in most organizations these rules are very formally structured and lie more or less static for years. Even when the first two sets of rules are amended based on business needs, economic trends and organizational strategies, the third set often remains static in spite of the fact that relationship structures and relational expectations change faster in the modern world.

Intra-organizational rules need to be based on negotiated contracts. In most organizations, though the rules are made based on a negotiated contract with the representatives of employees, these are neither amended nor contextualized according to their needs and requirements. Most of these rules lose relevance and thus, leaders interpret them according to their understanding and convenience. This results in a perception of unfairness among the team members.

When the rules are made, amended or interpreted to favour particular individuals, they lose legitimacy. There will be a tendency not to adhere to those rules.

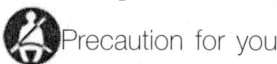Prescription for you, the boss

Leaders are people of action. They are the prime movers of change. To be a dynamic boss one should be prepared to formulate new rules to replace the obsolete ones.

Precaution for you

Breaking an obsolete rule may not be a good idea. But you could demonstrate to the bosses how a particular procedure is irrelevant and counter-productive.

Precept for the organizations

Rules that govern conduct and relationships (social embeddedness) within an organization should necessarily be formulated after a negotiated contract with the team members.

Rules within an organization should be made flexible to cater to the changing needs and requirements of the organization and members as well as surrounding conditions.

Any discretion given to the boss should not be aimed at arbitrary actions but only used to rescue the employee from the shackles of archaic and rigid rules.

The signs of recovery

When rules and procedures are continuously amended and reformed in tune with the requirements of all stakeholders, there is clarity of purpose, ease in implementation and less arbitrariness.

50

INEFFECTIVE BOSSES CREATE INEFFECTIVE ORGANIZATIONS

IN THE EARLIER 49 chapters we have discussed characteristic traits that are undesirable in leaders. Broadly, we can identify two categories of bosses: The 'wrong' bosses who have no good left and the 'good' bosses who do the wrong things. When we discussed the nasty, runaway, suspicious, petty, unethical, jealous, threatening and apathetic bosses, we were labelling them as wrong bosses. But when we dealt with the predecessor bashers, hyper-intelligent ones, braggarts and others we had hopes of recovery in spite of their aberrations. However, both categories are responsible for inefficiency and dissatisfaction within organizations.

Sick leaders make sick organizations

Look at the leadership of any organization. Who led it recently? Who is leading it now? You can get answers for the sickness or well-being of that organization. Sick bosses are responsible for sick organizations.

The nature, symptoms and conditions of sick bosses have been dealt with in this book. From the descriptions and discussions, we can identify 50 key traits of sick leaders. They are the following:

1. Ageist
2. Apathetic
3. Arrogant
4. Authoritarian
5. Autocratic

6. Blabbermouth
7. Braggart
8. Bureaucratic
9. Cognitive miser
10. Cranky
11. Credit-grabber
12. Cynical
13. Deceptive
14. Egocentric
15. Fault-finder
16. Gossip-monger
17. Hyper-intelligent
18. Immature
19. Impatient
20. Incompetent
21. Indecisive
22. Inscrutable
23. Jealous
24. Lazy
25. Moody
26. Nasty
27. Parochial
28. Petty
29. Please-all
30. Power-hungry
31. Predecessor basher
32. Prejudicial
33. Problem-averse
34. Procrastinator
35. Publicity hungry
36. Puppet-like
37. Rigid
38. Risk-averse
39. Rude
40. Stubborn

41. Suspicious
42. Sycophantic
43. Time bandit
44. Timid
45. Unapproachable
46. Unethical
47. Unfair
48. Unpredictable
49. Vindictive
50. Weak

Organizations with leaders possessing any of the above attributes create sick organizations. The nature, symptoms and conditions of sick organizations are given below.

1. A lot of negativity
2. Trust deficit
3. Poor resource management
4. Lack of innovation
5. Inappropriate supervision
6. Fights and jealousy among departments
7. Perception of unfairness
8. Lack of loyalty and commitment
9. Environment encouraging attrition
10. No change in working conditions
11. High stress levels
12. Little creativity
13. Little encouragement to excel
14. Lack of appreciation for excellence
15. Unsettled grievances from clients/public
16. Reduction in market value or social recognition
17. Less demand from fresh job applicants
18. Employees find happiness in criticizing the bosses
19. Frequent sharing of frustrations
20. Lack of organizational pride

It is unfortunate that certain organizations suffer under a series of ineffective bosses. Such organizations, in due course, absorb the traits of the leaders through established procedures, conventions, and practices. They may slowly develop a 'unique organizational behavioural pattern' that cannot be easily changed. Thus bosses can build or mar an organization.

Can a good boss bring in Organizational Citizenship Behaviour (OCB)?

It is found in research by Tal Yaffe and Ronit Kark that a leader who leads by example may promote his OCB directly and indirectly and contribute to the group OCB.[141] John T. Seaman Jr. and George David Smith have rightly said that 'as a leader strives to get people working together productively, communicating the history of the enterprise can instil a sense of identity and purpose and suggest the goals that will resonate'. But this should not end up as mere posturing. These should be scrupulously implemented. There are several empirical studies[142] that clearly point out that 'bad behaviour' in the organization can lead to 'bad behaviour' by individuals.

This is, in fact, a cyclical process. Bad individuals create bad organizations. Bad organizations in turn create an environment not only for bad leaders to thrive in but that may also initiate good ones into the rotten culture.

Do organizations pick up their own unique habits in the long run? Yes, they do. Sociologist Emile Durkheim who propounded the concept of 'collective consciousness' advocated that society has a mind of its own. According to him, the totality of common beliefs and sentiments of individuals in a society forms a unique determinate system. If Durkheim's view that the society has a conscience outside the realm of individuals can be accepted, then it can be argued that organizations are also characterized by their own unique identity, value system and behavioural uniqueness.

Habit is said to be a repeated behavioural pattern resulting from a thought process. The thought processes of individuals are influenced by several factors like their experiences, education, upbringing, behaviour of and interaction with their peers, kith and kin and exposure to media. Similarly, habits of organizations are rooted in their historicity, ideology, mission, vision, and habits of people manning them. Thus an organization is influenced by the habits that are dominant within the organization.

The vision and mission of an organization may have an important influence on organizational habits only if there is a strong consonance between the behaviour of the organization and its mission and vision statements. Every modern organization formulates a mission statement to impress its stakeholders. Bart[143] defines a mission statement as 'a formal written document intended to capture an organization's unique raison d'etre. It should answer such vital questions as: why do we exist, what is our real purpose and what are we trying to accomplish'. Many times, mission and vision statements stay in the idealistic realms and thus do not have any bearing on the way the organization acts and reacts. As such, many organizations function according to the ideologies, strategies and conduct of dominant groups or leading individuals within them. It could be the promoters, trade unions, long-serving senior executives or the government.

Organizational conscience

It would be appropriate to call the thought process and consequent behavioural pattern of an organization as emanating from 'organizational conscience'. The habits of an organization are a direct outcome of the organizational conscience, which itself is a direct result of the behavioural pattern of past bosses. If any individual or group of individuals has controlled an organization and had an overwhelming influence on the entire cultural fabric, then the behavioural pattern of that organization would be characterized by the personality traits, strategies and agenda of that individual or group.

While some organizational habits have a positive bearing on the growth and efficiency of an organization, others are an indication of a deeper malaise and would invariably contribute to ineffectiveness and decline.

Staying inscrutable by being superficially transparent

Leaders who are inefficient, inscrutable, and superficial would create organizations with the same traits. Here are some examples.

a. Reality is different from what is projected
The organization has its vision and mission clearly spelt out with the help of an articulate and versatile outsourcing team and displayed in the public domain. However, the vision and mission get blurred as time progresses and no one takes the initiative to revisit them. Though there could be a customer charter with tall promises, there won't be a provision to enforce the delivery of service. Websites become nothing but cobwebs because of lack of updates or messy presentation. Attractive front desks, grievance redressal centres, ombudsman systems and call centres become inaccessible, irresponsive and ineffective because of lack of competence, inadequate resources, absence of authority, and for want of proper action on feedback. Even more galling is the lack of will to serve.

b. Silo mentality
Each division within the organization works in silos and there is lack of co-ordination. Each division tries to maximize its benefits without bearing in mind the long-term consequences for the organization.

c. Risk-aversive behaviour
This is the habit of not taking certain steps that would benefit others but would expose any inefficiency or omission of the organization. Here, fear of failure looms large, killing any initiative. There is a paralysis in decision-making.

d. Boss-centrism
Some organizations have internal procedures and protocols heavily loaded in favour of the bosses. Competency takes a backseat in the face of seniority.

e. Insubordination
Though there are well-laid-out hierarchical levels within

the organization, lack of efficiency, ethical compliance, double standards and unfairness at top levels results in insubordination at all the other levels. There would be frequent episodes of blatant violation of the orders of superior authorities. Managers at each level may even criticize their superiors in front of subordinates, creating a culture of disobedience and mudslinging.

f. Organizational arrogance

There are many organizations that public and other stakeholders hate to interact with because of the perception of a culture of arrogance. Earlier, the organizations owned by governments and those in the public sector were accused of being arrogant. However, in the context of corporatization and mergers and acquisitions, many large private players who provide goods and services have also been blamed by the public as being rude and insensitive. There has been the emergence of a new breed of private bureaucrats.

g. Glory days syndrome

There are many organizations amidst us that continue to bask in their past glory, though they are either 'white elephants' or irrelevant now. A historical understanding of the organization is necessary, but not to the extent of eulogizing it without supporting evidence.

Many large organizations have a history of success, have exercised huge power and influence over many stakeholders, or brought substantial revenues to the state by way of revenue. They do not comprehend the far-reaching effects of the changes that are taking place. Instead of diversifying, modernizing or contextualizing in tune with the needs, priorities, and preferences of their customers, investors, state or the public, they continue to 'behave' big, without realizing that their foundations are breaking apart.

Epilogue

THANK YOUR BOSS FOR MAKING YOU A GOOD LEADER

We have seen various types of bosses and their characteristic traits in this book. Such bosses are very much around us. On introspection, we would have found that a few of the traits are a part of our personalities as well. Though the prescriptions, precautions, and precepts given at the end of each chapter can facilitate us to improve, we need to devise our own specific strategies to become an exemplary mentor for the team we lead—whether it is the family, the friend circle, the organization or the community. The mission is not only to become a leader who is recognized and respected, but also to be an individual who others find worth emulating.

Often, we are more interested in evaluating how our bosses behave with us, without introspecting our own behaviour towards those working under us. In our enthusiasm and determination to achieve what we want, we tend to extract a lot out of the people below us without assessing the limit to which they can be stretched.

A successful leader is one who has high levels of emotional, social, cultural and communication intelligence. With a humble approach, flexible attitude, honest intention, and empathetic response, anyone can become a role model for others. This will make us and the organizations we are affiliated with much more efficient, productive, happy and acceptable.

SCORE ANALYSIS

Exercise 1.1

Score: 8–10: Well aware. This is the ideal level. The awareness facilitates a better understanding of you and your situation while taking decisions that affect you personally

Score: 4–7: Reasonably aware. Moderate understanding of you could aid in taking decisions.

Score: 0–3: Very poor awareness: Worst scenario. Boss doesn't care about what you are. Decisions could be adverse for you.

Exercise 1.2

One could argue that it is not necessary that a boss should know the personal details of the people working directly under him. The point conveyed by the author is from a sociological point of view. To be a successful and acceptable leader by taking the appropriate decisions for the personal welfare of the employees, one needs to have an understanding of their background and interests.

Score: 16–20: Well aware. Ideal level. The clear awareness and understanding of the people below you facilitates you in taking decisions that might affect them personally.

Score: 6–15: Reasonably aware. Moderate understanding of your team could aid in taking decisions.

Score: 4–7: Very poor awareness. Worst-case scenario. You don't care what your subordinates are like.

Individuals at work are not inanimate objects. They carry with them problems, memories, aspirations and anxieties. A good leader attempts to have a holistic understanding of each team member and his background.

Exercise 2

Your communication quotient (CQ)
(Score sheet)

Qn	A	B	C	D	Notes
1	3	3	2	2	
2	1	2	3	5	
3	1	2	3	5	
4	1	2	4	5	
5	1	2	3	4	
6	1	2	3	5	
7	1	2	3	4	
8	4	3	2	1	
9	5	4	2	1	
10	1	1	5	5	
11	1	2	3	5	
12	2	3	3	3	
13	5	5	3	2	
14	1	2	3	5	
15	1	2	3	4	
16	1	2	3	3	
17	5	3	1	1	
18	1	2	3	5	
19	1	2	3	5	
20	5	4	3	1	
Column Total	(A)	(B)	(C)	(D)	Aggregate score (A+B+C+D)=

You have good speaking skills or writing ability. The above test doesn't assess these skills. It is exclusively aimed at assessing your communication intelligence.

Score: 70–90: Very high CQ (Ideal for a leader)

50–70: Moderate CQ (Good score. But improving communication skills will make you more effective and acceptable)

40–50: Low CQ (You need very systematic attitudinal and behavioural changes through training)

Below 40: Very low CQ (You need to understand that you have a serious problem in effective communication and may take the help of a counsellor/psychologist/communication consultant to improve your communication quotient)

Exercise 3

Assess your Cultural Intelligence
Circle your response

	A	B	C	D	E	Remarks
1	0	1	2	3	4	
2	4	3	2	1	0	
3	0	1	2	3	4	
4	4	3	2	1	0	
5	0	1	2	3	4	
6	0	1	2	3	4	
7	4	3	2	1	0	
8	4	3	2	1	0	
9	4	3	2	1	0	
10	4	3	2	1	0	
Total						

Score: 36–40: Very high cultural intelligence. You can successfully acculturate to any situation across geographic, linguistic and cultural boundaries. People love to be around you.

31–35: High cultural intelligence. You can get assimilated to foreign cultures very easily.

21–30: Moderate cultural intelligence. Since you do have a positive attitude towards understanding the situations you are in, you can overcome cross-cultural challenges through efforts.

11-20: Low cultural intelligence. You need to take deliberate steps to learn and unlearn to be successful in a new culture.

0-10: Very low cultural intelligence. Unless you transform drastically from the stereotyped notions and prejudices ingrained within, you may not be able to survive in a new cultural environment.

Exercise 5 Assessing your Emotional Intelligence

SCORE TABLE
A—Definitely/ B -Very likely/ C -likely/D—less likely/ E—never

	A Definitely	B Very likely	C Likely	D Less likely	E Never	Notes/Total score
1	1	2	3	4	5	
2	5	4	3	2	1	
3	1	2	3	4	5	
4	1	2	3	4	5	
5	1	2	3	4	5	
6	1	2	3	4	5	
7	1	2	3	4	5	
8	1	2	3	4	5	
9	1	2	3	4	5	
10	1	2	3	4	5	
11	1	2	3	4	5	
12	1	2	3	4	5	
13	2	2	2	2	2	
14	5	4	3	2	1	
15	1	2	3	4	5	
16	1	2	3	4	5	
17	1	2	3	4	5	
18	5	4	3	2	1	
19	5	4	3	2	1	
20	1	2	3	4	5	
Total						

Score analysis

Above 80: Very high emotional intelligence
Between 60 and 80: High emotional intelligence
Between 40 and 60: Moderate emotional intelligence
Between 20 and 40: Low emotional intelligence
Below 20: Very low emotional intelligence

Leaders need emotional intelligence in ample measure. It is the key to success for being a good leader. The test is not aimed at accurately calculating your Emotional Intelligence Score, but to provide awareness on various dimensions of emotional intelligence and how it is demonstrated in certain situations in professional life. In order to get an accurate score, I recommend that you undergo a comprehensive test covering all the attributes in detail. Those who scored more than 60 will be very successful as leaders. Persons who scored less than 40 need to radically change the way they approach people. They should look for an opportunity for professional training to improve their awareness about people and society so that they can develop their social qualities and be successful as leaders.

NOTES

1. One of the earliest theoretical positions on leaders and leadership are related to divine origin and also based on a notion that leaders are born and not made. It was commonly called the 'Great man theory of leadership'. Later sociologists like Herbert Spencer were the first to point out that leadership is a product of social experience. H. Spencer, *The Study of Sociology*, Appleton, New York, 1896.
2. Details can be found in Ralph M. Stogdill, *Handbook of Leadership: A Survey of Theory and Research*, New York, Free Press, 1974.
3. An excellent take on this is available in Barbara Kellerman, 'Leadership—Warts and All', *Harvard Business Review* on 'The Mind of the Leader', Harvard Business School Press, 2005, p. 9.
4. Undoubtedly, a better way to train people as leaders is by projecting ideal leadership attributes. An interesting read is, 'Ready-Now Leaders: Meeting Tomorrow's Business Challenges': Global Leadership Forecast 2014/15, www.ddiworld.com. Also see R. Bolden, J. Gosling, A. Marturano, and P. Dennison, 'A Review of Leadership Theory and Competency Frameworks', Centre for Leadership Studies, UK, June 2003. The scholars said that 'much has already been done to define what "qualities", "competencies", and "standards" should be sought from our leaders, but…this has done little to improve the quality of our leaders and leadership'.
5. The influence of the Weberian ideal type of 'rational-legal' leadership is very much evident in the leadership styles in organizations. Initially attributed to leaders in government, they became an integral constituent of medium and large corporate structures in the last few decades. It is assumed that in a rigid hierarchical and highly professional structure, the incumbents tend to become more impersonal as far as organizational objectives are concerned, but continue to be 'personal' as they weigh the costs and benefits for them. Thus, the assumption is that the people are happy as far as their needs are taken care of and the perception of attitudes of the bosses are never an area of serious concern.
6. Freud believed that the personality has three components called the Id (which functions in the irrational part of the mind), Ego (functions as the rational part of the mind), and the Superego (the moral part of the

mind). If these three components are well-balanced, then there would be reasonable mental health and stability in an individual.

7. Though the Trait Theory of Allport has been criticized by many scholars for its difficulty in measurement, it has given a new perspective to the theory of leadership. His own focus shifted in the later works, especially in his book *Becoming*. See G.W. Allport, 'Traits Revisited', *American Psychologist*, 21, 1966, pp. 1–10 and *Becoming: Basic Considerations for Psychology of Personality*, New Haven, Yale University Press, 1955.

8. These are a few scholars who analysed this perspective in detail: A. Zaleznik, 'Managers and leaders: Are they different?' *Harvard Business Review*, 55, 1977, pp. 67–68; M. Maccoby, *The Leader: A New Face for American Management*, New York: Ballantine, 1981; L.V. Berens, S.A. Cooper, L.K. Ernst, et al., *Quick Guide to the 16 Personality Types in Organizations*, Huntington Beach, CA: Telos, 2001. One of the positions of the psychodynamic approach is that the familial experiences in leadership have a bearing on the performance in the leadership roles one steps into later in life. (Leadership traits of father/mother/elder brother or self-leadership opportunity in family). This results in different types of leadership styles in the future: For example, familial, paternalistic and maternalistic.

9. For example, Micha Popper has identified several silent biases in discussions and research on leadership. Popper identified cognitive biases such as the fundamental attribution error, symbolic attribution error, attribution resulting from social distance, and cognitive cultural biases. (Micha Popper, 'Salient biases in discussion and research on leadership', in Ken W. Parry, and James R. Meindl (eds) *Grounding Leadership Theory and Research: Issues, Perspectives, and Methods*, Information Age Publishing Inc., 2002)

10. An integrated approach is imperative as there is an interplay of various factors. An example for this is, Bruce J. Avolio, 'Promoting more integrative strategies for leadership theory-building'. *American Psychologist*, 62, 2007, pp. 25-33.

11. M. Uhl-Bien and S. Ospina (eds), *Advancing Relational Leadership Research*, Charlotte, NC: Information Age Publishing 2014 and A. Cunlifee, and M. Eriksen, 'Relational Leadership', *Human Relations*, 64 (11), 2011, pp. 1425–49.

12. There is a theoretical basis to the belief that people below would emulate aggressive behaviour on top. Read, Simon Lloyd Restubog, Kristin L. Scott, Thomas J. Zagenczyk, 'When distress hits home: The role of contextual factors and psychological distress in predicting employees responses to abusive supervision', *Journal of Applied Psychology*, 96 (4), 2011, p. 713.

13 Some creative suggestions are given in this book: Jay Carter, *Nasty Bosses: How to Deal with Them without Stooping to Their Level*, McGraw Hill, 2004.
14 The concept is elaborated in this paper: 'Nonconscious relationship reactance: When significant others prime opposing goals', https://faculty.fuqua.duke.edu/~gavan/bio/GTF_articles/relationship_reactance_jesp_inpress.pdf
15 Thomas Hammock and Jack W. Brehm, Duke University, 'The attractiveness of choice alternatives when free to choose is eliminated by a social agent', *Journal of Personality*, 34 (4), pp. 546–54.
16 It is scientifically proved that productivity is linked to the leadership. Christina Boedker, 'Bosses are key to productivity', 5 September 2012, www.afr.com/p/national/wrok-space/bosses_are_key_to_productivity_qRnwlZdsPHyZAsKAWksWgJ)
17 Some scholars have found that the public engagement of leaders brings in visibility and productivity for the organization. J.P. Kotter. *The General Managers*, New York, Free Press, 1982; H. Mintzberg. *The Nature of Managerial Work*, New York, Harper & Row, 1973.
18 Read Edward L. Deci and Richard M. Ryan, *Intrinsic Motivation and Self-Determination in Human Behavior*, Springer, US, 1985.
19 Who wants to have an unpleasant situation in the workplace? See a study about how trust in workplaces brought happiness in http://www.greatplacetowork.com/about-us/about-us.
20 Drucker has written extensively on time management. See Peter Drucker, *The Effective Executive*, first edition. New York, Harper & Row, 1967.
21 Erik, Black, Jennifer Light, Nicole Paradise Black, and Linday Thompson, 'Online social network use by health care providers in a high traffic patient care environment', http://www.jmir.org/2013/5/e94/, 2013.
22 One very important consequence of unlimited and unrestricted social networking is the crossing of relationship boundaries. The study worth referring to is M. Meredith Skeels and Jonathan Grudin, 'When social networks cross boundaries: A case study of workplace use of Facebook and LinkedIn', http://research.microsoft.com/en-us/UM/People/jgrudin/publications/newwave/SocialNetworking2009.pdf.
23 Silence can be perceived as arrogance in many situations. Frank downward communication can bring in efficiency. Boris Groysberg and Michael Sind have made an interesting analysis in, 'Talk, Inc: How trusted leaders use conversation to power their organizations', *Harvard Business Review Press*, 2012.
24 Robert Greene's book may not be an ideal guide on exemplary leadership because of certain destructive and shrewd suggestions. The present

reference can be found on p. 120, *The 48 Laws of Power*, First South Asian Edition, Viva Books, 1999.

25 Quoted in Richard Boyatzis and Annie McKee, *Resonant Leadership*, Boston, Harvard Business School Press, 1998.

26 http://mobile.businessweek.com/articles/2012-12-31/new-years-resolutions-in-140-characters-or-less.

27 'Office Skills', September 1987, quoted in Dr S. Ramani and Professor V.S.R.D. Varma, *Humour and Productivity*, vol. 2, Vijaya & Venkat Publishers, Pune, 1989.

28 Chapter 65, Tao Te Ching, quoted in Diane Dreher, *The Tao of Personal Leadership*, Harper Collins, 1996. The book, drawing on leadership principles from the Tao Te Ching, Taoism, Buddhism and the martial arts shows how we can all become not only leaders but also courageous and resourceful individuals.

29 N.R. Narayana Murthy led Infosys for many decades and provided a leadership that inspired executives and managers worldwide. The letter referred to can be accessed on http://www.infosys.com/investors/reports-filings/annual-report/annual/Documents/AR-2011/Theme-Pages/goodbye_folks.html.

30 Intelligent, bright, and good leaders can also err in their decisions. See the study by Andrew Campbell, Jo Whitehead, and Sydney Finkelstein, 'Why good leaders make bad decisions', *Harvard Business Review*, February 2009, pp. 60–6.

31 Rosabeth Moss Kanter, *Confidence: How Winning Streaks and Losing Streaks Begin and End*, New York, Three Rivers Press, 2004.

32 E. Kelly et al. 'The detrimental effects of power on confidence, advice taking, and accuracy', doi:10.1016/j.obhdp.2011.07.006, 2011.

33 L. Yaniv, 'Receiving other people's advice: Influence and benefit', *Organizational Behaviour and Human Decision Processes*, 93, 2011, pp. 1–13.

34 People would like to be perfect though they do not always like being corrected repeatedly by others. An article by Etienne Benson is interesting in this context: 'The many faces of perfectionism', *Monitor Staff*, 34 (10), November 2003, p. 18.

35 Quoted in S. Ramani and V.S.R.D. Varma *Humour and Productivity*, vol. 2, Vijaya & Venkat Publishers, Pune, 1989.

36 Amy J.C. Cuddy, Matthew Kohut and John Neffinger in *Harvard Business Review, South Asia*, July–August 2013, p. 58.

37 Paul Babiak and Robert D. Hare, *Snakes in Suits: When Psychopaths Go to Work*, HarperBusiness, 2007.

38 One can gather views with a lot of clarity in the article titled 'The primacy of personality' in *Harvard Business Review*, 2012, p. 130.
39 D. Goleman, R. Boyatzis and A. McKee, *Primal Leadership: Realizing the Power of Emotional Intelligence*, Boston: Harvard Business School Press.
40 J. LeDoux, *The Emotional Brain: The Mysterious Underpinnings of Emotional Life*, New York, Simon and Schuster, 1996.
41 R. Davidson, D.C. Jackson and N.H. Kalin, 'Emotion, plasticity, context and regulation: Perspectives from affective neuroscience', *Psychological Bulletin*, 126(6), 2000 pp. 890–909.
42 E. Kelly et al. 'The detrimental effects of power on confidence, advice taking, and accuracy', doi:10.1016/j.obhdp.2011.07.006, 2011.
43 L. Yaniv, 'Receiving other people's advice: Influence and benefit', *Organizational Behaviour and Human Decision Processes*, 93, 2004, pp. 1–13.
44 Mohazin R. Banaji, Max H. Bazerman and Dolly Chugh, 'How (un)ethical are you?', in *On Managing People*, Boston, Harvard Business Review Press, 2011, pp. 157–73.
45 Reported in http://www.hrmagazine.co.uk/hro/news/1107069/managers-acting-unethical-ahead-cmi-study.
46 http://www.ey.com/Publication/vwLUAssets/Navigating_todays_complex_business_risks/$FILE/Navigating_todays_complex_business_risks.pdf.
47 The report can be accessed here: http://www.kroll.com/media/krl_fraudreport2013-14_usletterpress_revised_10182013.pdf.
48 S.E. Drouillard and B.H. Kleiner, '"Good" Leadership', *Management Development Review*, 9, 1996, pp. 30–3.
49 Testimony of Chairman Alan Greenspan: Federal Reserve Board's semi-annual monetary policy report to the Congress, before the Committee on Banking, Housing, and Urban Affairs, US Senate 16 July, 2002.
50 Y. Bersn, G. Shaul and D. Taly, 'CEO values, organizational culture and firm outcomes', *Journal of Organizational Behaviour*, 29, 2007, pp. 615–33.
51 The report can be accessed here: http://www.transparency.org/gcb2013/report.
52 http://www2.deloitte.com/in/en/pages/finance/articles/public-perception-of-anti-bribery-and-corruption-compliance-efforts.html.
53 'Who really makes the big decision in your company?' *Harvard Business Review*, December 2011, pp. 104–11.
54 The findings are reported in www.vodafone.co.uk/cs/groups/public/documents/content documents/uftst072735.pdf/.
55 Stuart L. Hart and Robert E. Quinn, *Human Relations*, 46, 1993, pp. 543–74. Also see, Robert L. Woolfolk and Robert G. Lord, 'Leader self-structure:

A framework for positive leadership', *Journal of Organizational Behaviour*, 30, 2009, pp. 269–90.
56 Linda D. Tillman, 'The power of no', www.speakforyourself.com/power_of_no.htm
57 Harriet Braiker, *The Disease to Please: Curing the People-pleasing Syndrome*, McGraw-Hill Professional, 2001.
58 The 80–20 rule attributed to the Italian economist and sociologist Vilfredo Pareto means that in every work situation, a few people are vital and many are trivial. The principle is applied by management scholars as 80 per cent of productivity comes from the work of 20 per cent of people.
59 Gianpiero Petriglieri and Mark Stein, 'The unwanted self: Projective identification in leaders' identity work', *Organization Studies*, 33 (9), 2012, p. 1221.
60 Jeffrey Sonnenfeld, *The Hero's Farewell: What Happens When CEOs Retire*, Oxford University Press, 1988.
61 Ron Maxie, Claire Raines and Bob Filipczak, *Generations at Work*, New York, AMACOM, 2000.
62 James W. Pennebaker, 'Your use of pronouns reveals your personality', *Harvard Business Review*, December 2011, pp. 32–33.
63 According to Ronnie Solan, 'the process of narcissistic self-love is activated by three absolute narcissistic needs: (a) to experience an altruistic state of well-being (homeostasis) in the familiar and constant state of self-love; (b) to separate the familiar self from the unfamiliar non-self; and (c) to integrate or befriend the unfamiliar yet "similar enough" non-self within the self in order to contain over-excitation.' See Ronnie Solan, 'Narcissistic fragility in the process of befriending the unfamiliar', *The American Journal of Psychoanalysis*, 58 (2), 1998, pp. 163–67.
64 Erika N. Carlson, Simine Vazire, Thomas F. Oltmanns, *Journal of Personality and Psychology*, 101 (1), 2011, pp. 185–201.
65 Joel Garfinkle, *Getting Ahead*, John Wiley & Sons, Inc, 2011.
66 http://mobile.businessweek.com/articles/2012-12-31/new-years-resolutions-in-140-characters-or-less.
67 G.W. Allport and H.S. Odbert. 'Trait-names: A psycho-lexical study.' *Psychological Monographs*, 47(211), 1936.
68 R.B. Cattell, *The Scientific Analysis of Personality*. Baltimore: Penguin Books, 1965.
69 H.J. Eysenck, 'Four ways five factors are not basic', *Personality and Individual Differences*, 13, 1992, pp. 667–73.
70 L.R. Goldberg, 'Language and individual differences: The search for universals in personality lexicons', in L. Wheeler (ed.), *Review of Personality*

and *Social Psychology, vol. 2*, Beverly Hills, CA, Sage, 1981.
71. R.R. McCrae, and P.T. Costa, 'Validation of the five-factor model of personality across instruments and observers', *Journal of Personality and Social Psychology*, 52, 1987, pp. 81–90.
72. Thomas and Margaret Melady, *Idi Amin Dada: Hitler in Africa*. Kansas City, 1977.
73. (http://www.cipd.co.uk/pm/peoplemanagement/b/weblog/archive/2013/04/22/almost-half-of-workers-find-bosses-threatening-survey-reveals.aspx).
74. FDA-Prospect evidence to the Senior Salaries Review Body October 2012, http://www.fda.org.uk/nmsruntime/saveasdialog.aspx?lID=5399&sID=7255).
75. http://www.smartcompany.com.au/growth/economy/3303-boss-fined-for-threatening-and-swearing-at-staff-member.html#.
76. David L. Dotlich and Peter B. Cairo, *Why CEOs Fail: The Ill Behaviours That Can Derail Your Climb to the Top and How to Change Them*, Jossey-Bass, 2003.
77. Reported in *Deccan Herald*, Bangalore, 27 February 2014, p. 11.
78. Edward P. Lazear, Kathryn L. Shaw and Christopher T. Stanton, 'The value of bosses', NBER Working Paper No. 18317, August 2012, www.nber.org/papers/w18317.
79. Morten T. Hansen, 'Three leadership skills that count', *Harvard Business Review South Asia* on point, August 2013–January 2014, p. 10.
80. According to the Mahabharata, in this stage an individual is in self-imposed celibacy, engaged in reflecting on the Vedas, silently reciting mantras obtained from his preceptor, observing rigid vows and controlling all senses.
81. The individuals who after studying all the Vedas and mantras, enter family life, beget children, enjoy pleasures and observe the ordinances of the scriptures.
82. After completing the stage of grahastha, the individual, with or without his wife, proceeds to the woods for the adoption of the mode called vanaprastha. He will retire from all worldly affairs.
83. This is the fourth and last stage where a man renounces the world and embraces the monastic way of life. He is no longer tempted by worldly pleasures or material possessions.
84. See 'Keys to engaging employees: "What drives employee engagement and why it matters?"' www.dalecarnegie.com/engaging-employees/, 2014.
85. A. Nyberg, et al. 'Managerial leadership and ischaemic heart disease among employees: the Swedish WOLF study.' Occup Environ Med 2008; DOI: 10.1136/oem.2008.039362.

86 To get very interesting resources on coping with bad bosses one could follow the postings in the website http://www.michellemcquaid.com/.
87 R.I. Sutton, *Good Boss, Bad Boss: How to be the Best... and Learn from the Worst,* New York, Business Plus, 2010.
88 R. Eisenberger, and F. Stinglhamber, *Perceived Organizational Support: Fostering Enthusiastic and Productive Employees,* Washington, DC: American Psychological Association Books. Also see, M. Gagne, and E.L. Deci, 'Self-determination theory and work motivation'. *Journal of Organizational Behavior,* 26, 2005, pp. 331–62, The study by N. Gillet and others has examined the relationships between perceived organizational support, perceptions of a supervisor's interpersonal style, psychological need satisfaction and need-thwarting and hedonic and eudemonic well-being. It was found that perceived organizational support and a supervisor's interpersonal style related to basic need satisfaction and need thwarting. See Nicolas Gillet, Jacques Fouquereau, Paul Brunault, and Philippe Colombat, 'The impact of organizational factors on psychological needs and their relations with well-being', *Journal of Business and Psychology,* 27 (4), December 2012, pp. 437–50.
89 http://www.examiner.com/article/research-shows-bad-bosses-are-bad-for-your-health.
90 American Psychological Association, 'Stress in America 2009'. http://www.apa.org/news/press/releases/stress-exec-summary.pdf, 2009.
91 M. Macik-frey, C, Q. James, and C.L. Cooper, 'Authentic leadership as a pathway to positive health', *Journal of Organizational Behaviour,* 30, 2009, pp. 453–58.
92 Mentioned by Mike Adams in 'Research finds bosses are driving employees crazy with weekend emails', tsminteractive.com/bosses_employees_weekend_emails/sept 21, 2012.
93 http://www.telegraph.co.uk/news/worldnews/europe/germany/10276815/Out-of-hours-working-banned-by-German-labour-ministry.html.
94 Dean C. Ludwig and Clinton O. Longenecker, 'The Bathsheba Syndrome: The Ethical Failure of Successful Leaders', *Journal of Business Ethics,* 12, 1993, pp. 265–73.
95 http://www.ericberne.com/games-people-play/.
96 You can see the details of his books and articles in http://www.kaaj.com/psych/.
97 You can read an informative article (draft) about Seshan in http://indiandemocracy08.berkeley.edu/docs/Gilmartin-OneDaysSultan.pdf.
98 An interesting article can be found in: http://indianeconomy.org/2007/10/12/when-manekshaw-confronted-indiras-cabinet/.

99. Dennis R. Young, 'Puppet leadership: An essay in honor of Gabor Hegyesi', Andrew Young School of Policy Studies, Working Paper 08-04, January 2008.
100. Michael Shea, *Leadership Rules*, Century, London, p. 2, 1990.
101. E. Vaara, and P. Monin, 'A recursive perspective on discursive legitimation and organizational action in mergers and acquisitions', *Organizational Science*, 21, 2010, pp. 3–22.
102. C. Chen and J.R. Meindl, 'The construction of leadership images in the popular press', *Administrative Science Quarterly*, 36, 1991, pp. 521–51.
103. Paresha Sinha, N. Kerr Inkson and James R. Barker, 'Committed to a failing strategy: Celebrity CEO, intermediaries, media and stakeholders in a co-created drama' *Organization Studies*, 33(2), 2012, p. 223–45.
104. R.E. Quinn, and K. Cameron, 'Organizational life cycles and the criteria of effectiveness.' *Management Science*, 29, 1983, pp. 63–77.
105. http://clomedia.com/articles/view/successful-leadership-transitions-boost-revenue.
106. Xueming Luo, Kanuri, V. and Andrews M. 'Why Too Long CEO Tenure May Hurt Firm Performance?' *Harvard Business Review*, March, 2013.
107. The book *48 Laws of Power* by Robert Greene may not be an ideal guide for ethical leadership. But it gives interesting tips to become successful leaders through the shortest route, Viking Penguin, 1998.
108. S. Robbins, Harvard Management Communication Letter, August 2001.
109. http://www.debonogroup.com/serious_creativity.php.
110. Blogs.hbr.org/cs/2012/08/are_you_sure_youre_not_a_bad_b_html, August 2012.
111. http://www.sas.com/jobs/corporate/index.html.
112. 'How to kill creativity?', *Harvard Business Review*, September–October 1998, p. 87.
113. G. Bennis and J. Thomas, *Geeks and Geezers: How Era, Values, and Defining Moments Shape Leaders*, Harvard Business School Press, Boston, 2002 p. 7.
114. *Ramapithecus* and *Proconsul* are earlier stages in human evolution much before *Homo sapiens*.
115. Gary Yukul, *Leadership in Organizations*, 5th edn, Prentice-Hall, 2002, p. 107.
116. www.sify.com/finance/interview with N R Narayanamurthy/.
117. E.H. Schein, *Career Dynamics: Matching Individual and Organizational Needs 1978*, Reading, M.A., Addison-Wesley and E.H. Schein. 'The role of founder in creating organizational culture', *Organizational dynamics*. Summer 1983, pp. 13–28.
118. The book *Goat Days* is a novel written by Joseph Benyamin, a Non-

Resident Indian who worked in a Gulf country. The English translation was published by Penguin (India).

119 http://rs.hudson.org/index.cfm?fuseaction=publication_details&id=416 The study was conducted in 1999.
120 http://www.mindtree.com/company/news/media-coverage/communication-key-reduce-attrition-mindtree.
121 http://www.klgates.com/files/publication/5ca1eda3-acd7-47e1-9431-6f0511d1e7e4/presentation/publicationattachment/ee2da30a-9843-4264-b182-f06d9d381051/corp_gov.pdf.
122 D.A. Victor, *International Business Communication*, Harper–Collins, New York, 1992.
123 E.S. Wibbeke, *Global Business Leadership*, 2009, Elsevier, p. 2.
124 http://www.dialogin.com/fileadmin/Files/User_uploads/executive_summary_delphi_study_results_sheridan_june_2005.pdf . Intercultural Leadership Competencies for U.S. Leaders. Also see Eileen Sheridan, in the Era of Globalization, dissertation, Doctor of Management, School of Advanced Studies University of Phoenix Online, 2005.
125 Reported in Harvard Business Review South Asia, January–February 2014, pp. 26–27.
126 Carmen Binnewies, Sabine Sonnentag and Eva J. Mojza, 'Daily performance at work: feeling recovered in the morning as a predictor of day-level job performance', *Journal of Organizational Behaviour*, 30, 2009, pp. 67–93.
127 A. Marcus-Newhall, W.C. Penderson, M. Carlson and N. Miller, 'Displaced aggression is alive and well: A meta-analytic review', *Journal of Personality and Social Psychology*, 78, 2000, pp. 670–89.
128 In *Harvard Business Review*, December, 2011.
129 *Harvard Business Review*, March 2012 in the column 'Interaction' p. 20.
130 http://tppserver.mit.edu/esd801/psds/11800988_Zaleznik_HBR.pdf.
131 John P. Kotter, 'What Leaders Really Do?' *Harvard Business Review Press*, 1999.
132 One can find a review of such studies in M.S. Cole, B. Heike and V. Bernd, 'Emotion as mediators of the relations between perceived supervisor support and psychological hardiness on employee cynicism', *Journal of Organizational Behaviour*, 27, 2006, pp. 463–84.
133 D. Goleman, *Emotional Intelligence: Why It Can Matter More than IQ*, New York, Bantam Books, 1995. Goleman who has researched extensively on the subject of emotional intelligence has argued that it is a better indicator than IQ in assessing a person's outstanding leadership qualities. (D. Goleman, *Working with Emotional Intelligence*, New York, Bantam Books, 1998.)

134 Daniel Goleman, 'What makes a leader?' in *On Leadership*, HBR Publishing Corporation, 2011, pp. 1–21.
135 R.B. Denhardt and J.V. Denhardt, *The Dance of Leadership*, New York, M.E. Sharpe, Inc, 2006, pp. 163, 175.
136 Debashis Chatterjee, *Leading Consciously: A Pilgrimage toward Self-mastery*, Viva Books, 1998, p. xix.
137 There are several standardized scales. Check the scale by Salovey and colleagues (MSCEIT Scale). Read also works by Lennart Sjoberg and Elisabeth Engelberg about measuring and validating the scales and the Emotional Intelligence scale by Schutte and others.
138 The readers may read Robert Alun Jones, *Emile Durkheim: An Introduction to Four Major Works,* Beverly Hills, CA, Sage Publications Inc., 1986.
139 Robert K. Merton has elaborated the subject in his book, *Social Theory and Social Structure,* Glencoe, IL, Free Press, 1957.
140 March Schulz and Zhou, *The Dynamics of Rules*, Stanford University Press, 2000.
141 Tal Yaffe, and Ronit Kark, 'Leading by example: the case of leader OCB', *Journal of Applied Psychology*, 96 (4), 2011, pp. 806–26.
142 See for example, Simon Lloyd S; Restubog, Kristin L. Scott, Thomas J. Zagenczyk 'When distress hits home: The role of contextual factors and psychological distress in predicting employees responses to abusive supervision', *Journal of Applied Psychology*, 96 (4), 2011, p. 714.
143 Christopher K. Bart, 'Exploring the application of mission statements on the world wide web', *Internet Research: Electronic Networking Applications and Policy*, II, 2001, pp. 360–68.